# WILLIAM COWPER

*Selected Poetry and Prose*

# WILLIAM COWPER

*Selected Poetry and Prose*

Edited by

## David Lyle Jeffrey

REGENT COLLEGE PUBLISHING
Vancouver, British Columbia

William Cowper: Selected Poetry and Prose
Introduction © 2007 by David Lyle Jeffrey
All rights reserved.

Published 2007 by Regent College Publishing
5800 University Boulevard, Vancouver, BC V6T 2E4 Canada
Web: www.regentpublishing.com
E-mail: info@regentpublishing.com

Regent College Publishing is an imprint of the Regent College
Bookstore. Views expressed in works published by Regent College
Publishing are those of the author and do not necessarily represent
the official position of Regent College <www.regent-college.edu>.

Selections from Cowper's letters are reprinted from Anna B.
McMahan, ed. *The Best Letters of William Cowper* (Chicago, 1893).

Library and Archives Canada Cataloguing in Publication Data

Cowper, William, 1731-1800
[Selections]
William Cowper : selected poems and prose /
William Cowper ; edited by David Jeffery.

Includes bibliographical references.

ISBN-10: 1-57383-228-6
ISBN-13: 9781573832281

1. Cowper, William, 1731-1800. 2. Poets, English—18th century--
Biography. 3. Cowper, William, 1731-1800—Correspondence.
4. Newton, John, 1725-1807—Correspondence. I. Jeffery, David, 1941-
II. Title.

PR3381.J42 2007          821.6          C2005-905463-8

For Mabel Brown
teacher by example, perseverant in grace

# CONTENTS

# INTRODUCTION

William Cowper has sometimes been described as "the great poet of the evangelical revival." While strictly speaking, the judgment is extreme (Charles Wesley would seem to have for the movement a greater claim), it is certainly true that Cowper was the most famous and respected of evangelical poets in the latter part of the century. With the emergence of his second major collection of secular poetry in 1785, he was in fact regarded by his critical contemporaries as perhaps the greatest poet of his generation. His place in the history of eighteenth-century spirituality owes, however, to work written well before this general fame was achieved; the story of how it came to be written offers, indeed, a fascinating insight into the spiritual history of the age.

Cowper's father was a priest in the Anglican church, himself the son of a notable judge, and a nephew of Earl Cowper, sometime lord chancellor of England. His mother, Ann Donne, who died in childbirth when Cowper was only six years of age, was a descendant of the family of John Donne, the seventeenth-century poet and dean of St. Paul's. William was the eldest of the only two children (of seven) to survive infancy. His family's position allowed him to be sent to Westminster School, where he was contemporary with Charles Churchill, the later to be impeached Warren Hastings, and Sir William Russell. In short, he had considerable early advantages. Yet these were not very well employed.

One of Cowper's early tutors was one Vincent Bourne, a brilliant but easy-going layabout of whom Cowper writes:

> I love the memory of Vinny Bourne. He was so good natured, and
> so indolent, that I lost more than I got by him; for he made me
> as idle as himself. He was such a sloven, as if he had trusted to

his genius as a cloak for everything that could disgust you in his person.*

The comment presages what was to become Cowper's besetting disposition—the idleness so common to the "advantaged" class of the period. He went on to study law at the Inner Temple, but there too he found birds of a feather with whom to flock, whiling away hours in the pubs, chop houses, and coffee houses instead of pursuing his preparation in law. As one of his biographers summarizes, "Cowper, throughout life, lacked personal initiative. He moved only in response to pressure from the outside."† This pattern, established so early, finally made him unable to respond well even under pressure. Perpetually aware as he was of professional unpreparedness, and haunted by guilt, he increasingly fled from any kind of responsibility. Thus, when a well-placed cousin offered him a political patronage appointment, he panicked at the prospect of the normal civil service examination. This precipitated three attempts at suicide, and a general nervous breakdown so severe that he was prevented from continuing in even the more modest position which he presently held. Just before Christmas of 1763, he was taken to a private madhouse supervised by Dr. Nathaniel Cotton at St. Albans.

As has often been pointed out, "Cowper's religious terrors were obviously the effect and not the cause of his madness."‡ Nevertheless, the form of his particular despair—an unshakeable conviction that he was eternally damned—made such a deep impression upon his agonized brain during the next five months that he was always in danger of relapsing toward its abyss, even after his conversion and return to the marginal emotional health he enjoyed thereafter. What followed—a sheltered life very near the edge but surrounded by the care of Christian "neighbors"—deserves at least a brief outline.

Cowper's brother John, a teaching fellow of what is now Corpus Christi College, Cambridge, undertook to find him permanent lodgings "post-recovery" and settled him in Huntingdon, nearby. Unable to live within his income (a small allowance from his family), he was forced to become a boarder with the priest of a local parish, Morley Unwin,

---

* Quoted in Gilbert Thomas, *William Cowper and the Eighteenth Century* (London: Nicholson and Watson, 1935), p. 75. The eighteenth-century "disease" of idleness is well described by Samuel Johnson in his essay on that subject in the Idler, no. 31.

† Thomas, p. 82.

‡ See, for example, the *Dictionary of National Biography* article on Cowper, p. 396.

and his wife Mary, who had offered to relieve him. This for a time entailed taking in also the servant Cowper had insisted on bringing with him from Dr. Cotton's. Much of his time with the Unwins was devoted to attending church services (twice daily), singing hymns, and participating in family prayers and the reading and discussion of spiritual writers. He gave the story of his conversion to one of his relatives in 1766 (though it was not published until 1816) and talked loosely about becoming, himself, a priest—much to the alarm of some of those who had been supporting him.

When in the early summer of 1767 Rev. Unwin died after a fall from his horse, Cowper stayed on with Mrs. Unwin, who had become to him something of a second mother. Shortly thereafter both came under the pastoral eye of John Newton. They became friends, and Newton moved them to a house near his parish church in Olney, even employing Cowper as a kind of lay curate in his parish work. Cowper attended services constantly and took part in prayer meetings and in visiting the sick and dying. This was in some sense the first real "work" he had been exposed to, and he seems in the beginning to have responded to it very well, becoming much respected in the parish. When his own brother lay dying at Cambridge, he went off to spend the last months with him, and during this time the brother himself was converted. (Cowper wrote a pamphlet called "Adelphi" about this experience, though it was not to be published until Newton released it in 1802.)

There was no greater influence on the life of Cowper from this point than that of John Newton. He became Cowper's spiritual director and, though sometimes subsequently maligned as an excessively Calvinistic influence upon the poet, Newton was actually a gentle instrument of grace to him in a diversity of ways. After Cowper's abortive engagement to Mary Unwin in 1773, and another relapse into depression, he was persuaded to spend a night in the Newton house—and then could not be talked into leaving for more than a year. Besides giving him employment which brought him into amiable and useful contact with others, Newton also encouraged Cowper's first interest in expressing his faith in the composition of poems and hymns. One of the first of these, on the verge of another serious attack of depression, was the well-known "God Moves in a Mysterious Way." Almost all of Cowper's 86 Olney Hymns (published in 1779 with Newton's own 280—including "Amazing Grace", "Zion, City of our God" and "How

Sweet the Name of Jesus Sounds") were composed between 1771 and 1773, during which time he was working closely with Newton. This was the real beginning of his poetic career; virtually everything that Cowper wrote of significance was composed after this time. Much of the work was read and editorially improved by Newton, and though Newton moved away to his London parish in 1780, he kept in regular contact with Cowper, always concerned for his emotional and spiritual health. In this sense, at least, the mature poetry of William Cowper was actually a foster child of John Newton's pastoral care.

After recovering from his depression, Cowper turned, in 1773, to gardening, small carpentry, and a much more systematic address to his writing as the necessary occupation he lacked. He was still supported by money from various relatives, and living still with Mrs. Unwin. A volume of his poems, including "Truth," "Hope" and "Charity" found in this volume, were written in a period of mere months in 1781, and appeared with a preface by Newton in 1782. Though not well received in London (the *Critical Review* called it a "dull sermon in very indifferent verse"), Benjamin Franklin wrote from France to say that he liked it very much, and it was happily received by Hannah More, who was delighted to discover, as she put it, "a poet...[she] could read on Sunday."*

It is now difficult to read Cowper's longer poems with the understanding they merit, especially those that meditate on theological subjects in the context of eighteenth-century life and political issues. To afford the twenty-first century reader some modest assistance in this regard, I have included footnotes to prominent biblical allusions and to eighteenth-century personages for these poems. No such effort can be sufficient for everyone. To take but one example: Cowper quotes from Milton's *Paradise Lost* almost as frequently as he alludes to the Bible; he regarded Milton as the supreme voice in English poetry (indeed thought him never to have been "equaled, unless perhaps by Virgil"); he read Milton aloud during the evening to Mrs. Unwin; and, when Samuel Johnson's *Lives of the Poets* (1779) seem to slight Milton as a poet, Cowper penned an impassioned rebuttal in a letter to William Unwin, Mary's son. For Cowper, Milton's poetry was perpetually the main music in his inner ear, and while no one thoroughly familiar

---

*    From the *Letters*, quoted in M.G. Jones, *Hannah More* (New York: Greenwood, 1968), p. 90. Cowper developed a comparably strong appreciation for More's writing, and a literary friendship of considerable mutual significance ensued.

with *Paradise Lost* can fail to note its enormous influence on his poetic development during the 1780s in particular, it has not seemed practical in an edition of this type to annotate these allusions.

A curious acquaintance of this period, Lady Austen, encouraged him to experiment in blank verse, which he did in his long poem, "The Task." This appeared with the humorous and very successful "John Gilpin" in 1785. One bookseller alone sold six thousand copies, and immediately Cowper was catapulted into fame. Almost as immediately, he was being asked about how soon his next book would appear. He undertook a translation of Homer—a conservative project and one that promised financial success. But the pressures on him were again too much; following a move to a "better house" in 1787, he had another bout of depression lasting six months, during which time he tried to hang himself again. Mrs. Unwin accidentally entered his room and cut him down. Although his recovery was rapid, he lived from this time forward in relative emotional fragility. His translation of Homer did not appear until 1791. He began but did not finish an edition of Milton, and much of the balance of his life was consumed in the mere management of necessity. His last original poem, written two years before his death, was "The Castaway"—a work which expresses as much spiritual uncertainty as his Olney Hymns express and experience a measure of grace. Cowper thus remains an enigmatic and troubling figure in this period, at once a witness to the healing spirit of Christ in those who ministered to him and an example of the destructive psychological forces at work in the society in which he lived. In an age which looked for the well-wrought urn, he was in truth a broken vessel, yet it was given to him to compose some of the most telling spiritual poetry of the period and so become an instrument of grace—grace beyond the reach of art, and speaking a peace he was not himself fully able to know.

# FROM
# MEMOIR OF THE EARLY LIFE OF
# WILLIAM COWPER, ESQ.
# WRITTEN BY HIMSELF

*In this vivid narrative, of which only an excerpt can be included here, Cowper describes his earliest memories, his unhappy, bullied years at Westminster School, his indolence during several years of unproductive study of law at the Inner Temple, and his resulting insecurity at being called to the bar in 1754. He then relates, in painful detail, the fits of depression which overtook him upon his conviction that he was not in fact qualified for the government position he had acquired by family influence and party patronage. The depression culminated in three unsuccessful attempts at suicide—one by an overdose of the drug laudanum, another a thwarted attempt to throw himself from a London bridge, and the third an attempted hanging in his room—followed in turn by loss of his job and a complete breakdown requiring his removal to a private hospital for the mentally ill. We pick up Cowper's story at a point just after his efforts at suicide.*

My sins were now set in array against me and I began to see and feel that I had lived without God in the world. As I walked to an fro in my chamber, I said within myself, "There never was so abandoned a wretch, so great a sinner." All my worldly sorrows seemed as though they had never been, the terrors which succeeded them seeming so great and so much more afflicting. One moment I thought myself shut out from mercy by one chapter; the next, by another. The sword of the Spirit seemed to guard the tree of life from my touch, and to flame against me in every avenue by which I attempted to approach it. I particularly remember that the parable of the barren fig-tree was to me an inconceivable source of anguish; I applied it to myself with a strong persuasion in my mind that when the Saviour pronounced a

15

curse upon it, He had me in his eye and pointed that curse directly at me.

I turned over all Archbishop Tillotson's sermons in hopes of finding one upon the subject, and consulted my brother upon the true meaning of it—desirous, if possible, to obtain a different interpretation of the matter than my evil conscience would suffer me to fasten on it. "O Lord, thou didst vex me with all thy storms, all thy billows went over me; thou didst run upon me like a giant in the night season, thou didst scare me with visions in the night season."

In every book I opened, I found something that struck me to the heart.

I remember taking up a volume of Beaumont and Fletcher,* which lay upon the table in my kinsman's lodgings, and the first sentence which I saw was this: "The justice of the gods is in it." My heart instantly replied, "It is a truth," and I cannot but observe that as I found something in every author to condemn me, so it was the first sentence, in general, I pitched upon. Everything preached to me, and everything preached the curse of the law.

I was now strongly tempted to use laudanum not as a poison but as an opiate to compose my spirits, to stupify my awakened and feeling mind which was harassed with sleepless nights and days of uninterrupted misery. But God forbad it, who would have nothing to interfere with the quickening work He had begun in me. Neither the lack of rest nor continued agony of mind could bring me to the use of it; I hated and abhorred the very smell of it.

I never went into the street but I thought the people stood and laughed at me and held me in contempt, and I could hardly persuade myself other than that the voice of my conscience was loud enough for everyone to hear it. They who knew me seemed to avoid me, and if they spoke to me seemed to do it in scorn. I bought a ballad of one who was singing it in the street because I thought it was written about me.

I dined alone, either at the tavern where I went in the dark or at the chop-house where I always took care to hide myself in the darkest corner of the room. I slept generally an hour in the evening, but it was only to be terrified in dreams. When I awoke it was some time before I could walk steadily through the passage into the dining room. I reeled

---

\* Francis Beaumont and John Fletcher, late Elizabethan dramatists, whose plays had been revived and republished during the Restoration period.

and staggered like a drunk man. The eyes of man I could not bear, but when I thought that the eyes of God were upon me (which I felt assured of) it gave me the most intolerable anguish. If, for a moment, a book or a companion stole away my attention from myself, a flash from hell seemed to be thrown into my mind immediately, and I said within myself, "What are these things to me, who am damned?" In a word, I saw myself a sinner altogether, and every way a sinner, but I saw not yet a glimpse of the mercy of God in Jesus Christ.

The capital engine in all the artillery of Satan had not yet been employed against me; already overwhelmed with despair, I was not yet sunk into the bottom of the gulf. This was a fit season for the use of it, and accordingly I was set to inquire whether I had not been guilty of the unpardonable sin, and was presently persuaded that I had.

A failure to respond to the mercies of God at Southampton, on the occasion above mentioned,* was represented to me as the sin against the Holy Ghost. No favorable construction of my conduct in that instance, no argument of my brother (who was now with me), nothing he could suggest in extenuation of my offences, could gain a moment's admission. Satan furnished me so readily with weapons against myself that neither scripture nor reason could undeceive me. Life appeared to me now preferable to death only because it was a barrier between me and everlasting burnings.

My thoughts in the day became still more gloomy, and my night visions more dreadful. One morning, as I lay between sleeping and waking, I seemed to myself to be walking in Westminster Abbey, waiting till prayers should begin. Presently I thought I heard the minister's voice, and hastened towards the choir. But just as I was upon the point of entering, the iron gate under the organ was flung in my face with a jar that made the Abbey ring; the noise awoke me, and a sentence of excommunication from all the churches upon earth could not have been so dreadful to me as the interpretation which I could not avoid putting upon this dream.

Another time I seemed to pronounce to myself, "Evil be thou my good." I verily thought that. I had adopted that hellish sentiment, it

---

*     Earlier in the narrative, Cowper records that standing on a beach, weighted down with depression, he had been transformed in spirit by the sun suddenly breaking through, which he took at once to be a sign of God's mercy toward him. Later, however, he passed off this incident as nothing more than coincidence. Now he has begun to fear that this rejection of his initial response may have amounted to a deliberate refusal of grace.

seemed to come so directly from my heart. I rose from bed to look for my prayer book and having found it endeavored to pray, but immediately experienced the impossibility of drawing nigh to God unless He first drew nigh to us. I made many passionate attempts towards prayer, but failed in all.

Having an obscure notion about the efficacy of faith, I resolved upon an experiment to prove whether I had faith or not. For this purpose I resolved to repeat the Creed. When I came to the second statement of it* all traces of the former were struck out of my memory, nor could I recollect one syllable of the matter. While I endeavored to recover it, and when just upon the point, I perceived a sensation in my brain like a tremulous vibration in all the fibres of it. By this means, I lost the words in the very instant when I thought to have laid hold of them. This threw me into an agony, but growing a little calmer I made an attempt for the third time; here again I failed in the same manner as before.

I considered it as a supernatural interposition to inform me that, having sinned against the Holy Ghost, I had no longer any interest in Christ or in the gifts of the Spirit. Being assured of this with the most rooted conviction, I gave myself up to despair. I felt a sense of burning in my heart like that of real fire, and concluded it was an earnest of those eternal flames which would soon receive me. I laid myself down howling with horror while my knees smote against each other.

In this condition my brother found me, and the first words I spoke to him were, "Oh, brother, I am damned! Think of eternity, and then think what it is to be damned!" I had, indeed, a sense of eternity impressed upon my mind, which seemed almost to amount to a full comprehension of it.

My brother, pierced to the heart with the sight of my misery, tried to comfort me, but all to no purpose. I refused comfort, and my mind appeared to me in such colors that to administer comfort to me was only to exasperate me and to mock my fears.

At length, I remembered my friend Martin Madan, and sent for him. I used to think him an enthusiast, but now seemed convinced that if there was any balm in Gilead, he must administer it to me. On former occasions, when my spiritual concerns had at any time occurred to me, I thought likewise on the necessity of repentance.

---

*    The section beginning, "And in one Lord Jesus Christ . . . ."

I knew that many persons had spoken of shedding tears for sin, but when I asked myself whether the time would ever come when I should weep for mine, it seemed to me that a stone might sooner do it.

Not knowing that Christ was exalted to give repentance, I despaired of ever attaining it. My friend came to me; we sat on the bedside together and he began to declare to me the Gospel. He spoke of original sin, and the corruption of every man born into the world, whereby everyone is a child of wrath. I perceived something like hope dawning in my heart. This doctrine set me more on a level with the rest of mankind and made my condition appear less desperate.

Next he insisted on the all-atoning efficacy of the blood of Jesus and his righteousness for our justification. While I heard this part of his discourse, and the scriptures upon which he founded it, my heart began to burn within me; my soul was pierced with a sense of my bitter ingratitude to so merciful a Saviour—and those tears which I thought impossible burst forth freely. I saw clearly that my case required such a remedy, and had not the least doubt within me but that this was the Gospel of salvation.

Lastly, he urged the necessity of a lively faith in Jesus Christ, not an assent only of the understanding but a faith of application, an actual laying hold of it and embracing it as a salvation wrought out for me personally. Here I failed and deplored my want of such a faith. He told me it was the gift of God which he trusted He would bestow upon me. I could only reply, "I wish He would"—a very irreverent petition, but a very sincere one, and such as the blessed God in his due time was pleased to answer.

My brother, finding that I had received consolation from Mr. Madan, was very anxious that I should take the earliest opportunity of conversing with him again, and for this purpose pressed me to go to him immediately. I was for putting it off, but my brother seemed impatient of delay and at length prevailed on me to set out. I mention this, to the honor of his candor and humanity, which would suffer no difference of sentiments to interfere with them. My welfare was his only object, and all prejudices fled before his zeal to procure it. May he receive, for his recompence, all that happiness the Gospel which I then first became acquainted with is alone able to impart.

Easier, indeed, I was, but far from easy. The wounded spirit within me was less in pain, but by no means healed. What I had experienced was but the beginning of sorrows, and a long train of still greater terrors was at hand. I slept my three hours well and then awoke with ten times a stronger alienation from God than ever. Satan plied me closely with horrible visions and more horrible voices. My ears rang with the sound of torments that seemed to await me. Then did the pains of hell get hold on me, and before daybreak the very sorrows of death encompassed me. A numbness seized upon the extremities of my body, and life seemed to retreat before it; my hands and feet became cold and stiff, a cold sweat stood upon my forehead, my heart seemed at every pulse to beat its last, and my soul to cling to my lips as if on the very brink of departure. No convicted criminal ever feared death more, or was more assured of dying.

At eleven o'clock, my brother called upon me, and in about an hour after his arrival that distemper of mind which I had so ardently wished for actually seized me.

While I traversed the apartment in the most horrible dismay of soul, expecting every moment that the earth would open her mouth and swallow me, my conscience scaring me, the avenger of blood pursuing me, and the city of refuge out of reach and out of sight, a strange and horrible darkness fell upon me. If it were possible that a heavy blow could light on the brain without touching the skull, such was the sensation I felt. I clapped my hand to my forehead and cried aloud through the pain it gave me. At every stroke, my thoughts and expressions became more wild and incoherent; all that remained clear was the sense of sin and the expectation of punishment. These kept undisturbed possession all through my illness without interruption or abatement.

My brother instantly observed the change, and consulted with my friends on the best manner to dispose of me. It was agreed among them that I should be carried to St. Alban's, where Dr. Cotton kept a house for the reception of such patients and with whom I was known to have a slight acquaintance. Not only his skill as a physician recommended him to their choice but his well-known humanity and sweetness of temperament. It will be proper to draw a veil over the secrets of my prison-house; let it suffice to say that the low state of body and mind to which I was reduced was perfectly well calculated to humble the natural vainglory and pride of my heart.

These are the efficacious means which Infinite Wisdom thought meet to make use of for that purpose. A sense of self-loathing and abhorrence ran through all my insanity. Conviction of sin, and expectation of instant judgement never left me from the 7th of December, 1763, until the middle of the July following. The accuser of the brethren was ever busy with me night and day, bringing to my recollection in dreams the commission of long-forgotten sins and charging upon my conscience things of an indifferent nature as atrocious crimes.

All that passed in this long interval of eight months may be classed under two headings, conviction of sin and despair of mercy. But, blessed be the God of my salvation for every sigh I drew, for every tear I shed, since it pleased Him thus to judge me here that I might not be judged hereafter.

After five months of continual expectation that the divine vengeance would plunge me into the bottomless pit, I became so familiar with despair as to have contracted a sort of hardiness and indifference as to the event. I began to persuade myself that while the execution of the sentence was suspended, it would be in my interest to indulge a less horrible train of ideas than I had been accustomed to muse upon. "Eat and drink, for tomorrow thou shalt be in hell" was the maxim on which I proceeded. By this means, I entered into conversation with the Doctor, laughed at his stories and told him some of my own to match them, still, however, carrying a sentence of irrevocable doom in my heart.

He observed the seeming alteration with pleasure. Believing, as well he might, that my smiles were sincere, he thought my recovery well nigh completed. But these were, in reality, like the green surface of a morass, pleasant to the eye but a cover for nothing but rottenness and filth. The only thing that could promote and effectuate my cure was yet wanting—an experimental knowledge of the redemption which is in Christ Jesus.

I remember, about this time, a diabolical species of regret that found harbor in my wretched heart. I was sincerely sorry that I had not seized every opportunity of giving scope to my wicked appetites, and even envied those who, being departed to their own place before me, had the consolation to reflect that they had well earned their miserable inheritance by indulging their sensuality without restraint. Oh, merciful God What a tophet of pollution is the human soul and wherein do we differ from the devils, unless thy grace prevent us!

In about three months more (July 25, 1764), my brother came from Cambridge to visit me. Dr. C. having told him that he thought me greatly amended, he was rather disappointed at finding me almost as silent and reserved as ever, for the first sight of him struck me with many painful sensations both of sorrow for my own remediless condition and envy of his happiness.

As soon as we were left alone, he asked me how I found myself. I answered, "as much better as despair can make me." We went together into the garden. Here, on expressing a settled assurance of sudden judgement, he protested to me that it was all a delusion, and protested so strongly that I could not help giving some attention to him. I burst into tears and cried out, "if it be a delusion, then am I the happiest of beings." Something like a ray of hope was shot into my heart, but still I was afraid to indulge it. We dined together and I spent the afternoon in a more cheerful manner. Something seemed to whisper to me every moment, "still there is mercy."

Even after he left me, this change of sentiment gathered ground continually, yet my mind was in such a fluctuating state that I can only call it a vague presage of better things at hand, without being able to assign a reason for it. The servant observed a sudden alteration in me for the better, and the man, whom I have ever since retained in my service, expressed great joy on the occasion.

I went to bed and slept well. In the morning, I dreamed that the sweetest boy I ever saw came dancing up to my bedside; he seemed just out of leading-strings, yet I took particular notice of the firmness and steadiness of his tread. The sight affected me with pleasure, and served at least to harmonize my spirits so that I awoke for the first time with a sensation of delight on my mind. Still, however, I knew not where to look for the establishment of the comfort I felt; my joy was as much a mystery to myself as to those about me. The blessed God was preparing me for the clearer light of his countenance by this first dawning of that light upon me.

Within a few days of my first arrival at St. Alban's, I had thrown aside the Word of God, as a book in which I had no longer any interest or portion. The only instance in which I can recollect reading a single chapter was about two months before my recovery. Having found a Bible on the bench in the garden,* I opened upon the 11th of St. John, where Lazarus is raised from the dead, and saw so much benevolence,

---

* This passage evokes the powerful parallel of St. Augustine's conversion, described in Book 8 of his *Confessions*, where he too comes upon a Bible on a bench in a garden, picks it up and recognizes that the work of redemption in Christ applies to him.

mercy, goodness and sympathy with miserable man in our Saviour's conduct that I almost shed tears even after the relation, little thinking that it was an exact type of the mercy which Jesus was on the point of extending towards myself. I sighed, and said, "Oh that I had not rejected so good a Redeemer, that I had not forfeited all his favors!" Thus was my heart softened, though not yet enlightened. I closed the book, without intending to open it again.

Having risen with somewhat of a more cheerful feeling, I repaired to my room, where breakfast waited for me. While I sat at table, I found the cloud of horror which had so long hung over me was every moment passing away, and every moment came fraught with hope. I was continually more and more persuaded that I was not utterly doomed to destruction. The way of salvation was still, however, hid from my eyes, nor did I see it at all clearer than before my illness. I only thought that if it would please God to spare me, I would lead a better life, and that I would yet escape hell if a religious observance of my duty would secure me from it.

Thus may the terror of the Lord make a Pharisee, but only the sweet voice of mercy in the Gospel can make a Christian.

But the happy period which was to shake off my fetters and afford me a clear opening of the free mercy of God in Christ Jesus was now arrived. I flung myself into a chair near the window and, seeing a Bible there, ventured once more to apply to it for comfort and instruction. The first verse I saw was the 25th of the third chapter of Romans: "Whom God hath set forth to be a propitiation through faith in his blood, to declare his righteousness for the remission of sins that are past, through the forbearance of God."

Immediately I received strength to believe it, and the full beams of the Sun of Righteousness shone upon me. I saw the sufficiency of the atonement He had made, my pardon sealed in his blood, and all the fullness and completeness of his justification. In a moment I believed, and received the Gospel. Whatever my friend Madan had said to me long before revived in all its clearness, with demonstration of the Spirit and with power. Unless the Almighty arm had been under me, I think I should have died with gratitude and joy. My eyes filled with tears, and my voice choked with transport, I could only look up to heaven in silent fear, overwhelmed with love and wonder. But the work of the Holy Ghost is best described in his own words; it is "joy unspeakable, and full of glory." Thus was my heavenly Father in Christ

Jesus pleased to give me the full assurance of faith, and out of a strong, stony, unbelieving heart, to raise up a child unto Abraham. How glad should I now have been to have spent every moment in prayer and thanksgiving!

I lost no opportunity of repairing to a throne of grace, but flew to it with an earnestness irresistible and never to be satisfied. Could I help it? Could I do otherwise than love and rejoice in my reconciled Father in Christ Jesus? The Lord had enlarged my heart, and I ran in the way of his commandments. For many succeeding weeks, tears were ready to flow if I did but speak of the Gospel or mention the name of Jesus. To rejoice day and night was all my employment. Too happy to sleep much, I thought it was but lost time that was spent in slumber. Oh that the ardor of my first love had continued! But I have known many a lifeless and unhallowed hour since, long intervals of darkness interrupted by short returns of peace and joy in believing.

My physician, ever watchful and apprehensive for my welfare, was now alarmed lest the sudden transition from despair to joy should terminate in a fatal frenzy. But "the Lord was my strength and my song, and was become my salvation," I said, "I shall not die, but live, and declare the works of the Lord; he has chastened me sore, but not given me over unto death. O give thanks unto the Lord, for his mercy endureth forever.

In a short time, Dr. C. became satisfied, and acquiesced in the soundness of my cure, and much sweet communion I had with him concerning the things of our salvation. He visited me every morning while I stayed with him, which was nearly twelve months after my recovery, and the Gospel was the delightful theme of our conversation.

No trial has befallen me since except what might be expected in a state of warfare. Satan, indeed, has changed his battery. Before my conversion, sensual gratification was the weapon with which he sought to destroy me. Being naturally of an easy, quiet disposition, I was seldom tempted to anger; yet it is that passion which now gives me the most disturbance, and occasions the sharpest conflicts. But Jesus being my strength, I fight against it, and if I am not conqueror, yet I am not overcome. . . .

# POEMS

# TRUTH

*Pensantur trutinâ—Hor. Lib. ii. Ep. 1.*

Man, on the dubious waves of error toss'd,
His ship half foundered, and his compass lost,
Sees, far as human optics may command,
A sleeping fog, and fancies it dry land:
Spreads all his canvas, every sinew plies;
Pants for it, aims at it, enters it, and dies!
Then farewell all self-satisfying schemes,
His well-built systems, philosophic dreams;
Deceitful views of future bliss, farewell!
He reads his sentence at the flames of hell.

   Hard lot of man—to toil for the reward
Of virtue, and yet lose it! Wherefore hard?—
He that would win the race must guide his horse
Obedient to the customs of the course;
Else, though unequalled to the goal he flies,
A meaner than himself shall gain the prize.
Grace leads the right way: if you choose the wrong,
Take it, and perish; but restrain your tongue.
Charge not, with light sufficient, and left free,
Your wilful suicide on God's decree.

   Oh how unlike the complex works of man,
Heaven's easy, artless, unencumbered plan!
No meretricious graces to beguile,
No clustering ornaments to clog the pile;
From ostentation, as from weakness, free,
It stands like the cerulian arch we see,
Majestic in its own simplicity.
Inscribed above the portal, from afar

Conspicuous as the brightness of a star,
Legible only by the light they give,
Stand the soul-quick'ning words—BELIEVE, AND LIVE!*
Too many, shocked at what should charm them most,
Despise the plain direction, and are lost.
Heaven on such terms! (they cry, with proud disdain)
Incredible, impossible, and vain!—
Rebel, because 'tis easy to obey;
And scorn, for its own sake, the gracious way.
These are the sober, in whose cooler brains
Some thought of immortality remains;
The rest, too busy, or too gay to wait
On the sad theme, their everlasting state,
Sport for a day, and perish in a night;
The foam upon the waters not so light.

    Who judged the Pharisee? What odious cause
Exposed him to the vengeance of the laws?
Had he seduced a virgin, wronged a friend,
Or stabbed a man to serve some private end?
Was blasphemy his sin? Or did he stray
From the strict duties of the sacred day?
Sit long and late at the carousing board?
(Such were the sins with which he charged his Lord.)
No—the man's morals were exact. What then?
'Twas his ambition to be seen of men;
His virtues were his pride, and that one vice
Made all his virtues gewgaws of no price;
He wore them as fine trappings for a show;
A praying, synagogue-frequenting, beau.†

    The self-applauding bird, the peacock, see—
Mark what a sumptuous Pharisee is he!
Meridian sun-beams tempt him to unfold
His radiant glories, azure, green, and gold:
He treads as if, some solemn music near,
His measured step were governed by his ear;

---

\*     Cf. John 6:4; 1 Tim 1:16.
†     Cf. Luke 18:9-14.

And seems to say—Ye meaner fowl, give place;
I am all splendour, dignity, and grace!

Not so the pheasant on his charms presumes;
Though he, too, has a glory in his plumes.
He, Christian-like, retreats with modest mien
To the close copse, or far-sequestered green,
And shines, without desiring to be seen.
The plea of works, as arrogant and vain,
Heaven turns from with abhorrence and disdain;
Not more affronted by avowed neglect,
Than by the mere dissembler's feigned respect.
What is all righteousness that men devise?
What—but a sordid bargain for the skies!
But Christ as soon would abdicate his own,
As stoop from heaven to sell the proud a throne.

His dwelling a recess in some rude rock;
Book, beads, and maple-dish, his meagre stock;
In shirt of hair and weeds of canvas dressed,
Girt with a bell-rope that the Pope has bless'd;
Adust with stripes told out for ev'ry crime,
And sore tormented, long before his time;
His prayer preferred to saints that cannot aid,
His praise postponed, and never to be paid;
See the sage hermit, by mankind admired,
With all that bigotry adopts inspired,
Wearing out life in his religious whim,
Till his religious whimsy wears out him.
His works, his abstinence, his zeal allowed,
You think him humble—God accounts him proud.
High in demand, though lowly in pretence,
Of all his conduct this the genuine sense—
My penitential stripes, my streaming blood,
Have purchased heaven, and proved my title good.

Turn eastward now, and fancy shall apply
To your weak sight her telescopic eye.
The Bramin kindles on his own bare head

The sacred fire—self-torturing his trade!
His voluntary pains, severe and long,
Would give a barb'rous air to British song;
No grand inquisitor could worse invent,
Than he contrives, to suffer, well content.

Which is the saintlier worthy of the two?
Past all dispute, yon anchorite, say you.
Your sentence* and mine differ. What's a name?
I say the Bramin has the fairer claim.
If sufferings, Scripture no where recommends,
Devised by self, to answer selfish ends,
Give saintship, then all Europe must agree
Ten starveling hermits suffer less than he.

The truth is (if the truth may suit your ear,
And prejudice have left a passage clear)
Pride has attained a most luxuriant growth,
And poisoned ev'ry virtue in them both.
Pride may be pampered while the flesh grows lean;
Humility may clothe an English dean;
That grace was Cowper's†—his, confessed by all—
Though placed in golden Durham's second stall.
Not all the plenty of a bishop's board,
His palace, and his lacqueys, and "My Lord,"
More nourish pride, that condescending vice,
Than abstinence, and beggary, and lice;
It thrives in misery, and abundant grows:
In misery fools upon themselves impose.

But why before us Protestants produce
An Indian mystic, or a French recluse?
Their sin is plain; but what have we to fear,
Reformed and well instructed? You shall hear.

Yon ancient prude, whose withered features shew

*     i.e., "judgment"
†     Spencer Cowper (1713-74), Dean of Durham Cathedral, hence in the second stall
because second to the Bishop.

She might be young some forty years ago,
Her elbows pinioned close upon her hips,
Her head erect, her fan upon her lips,
Her eyebrows arched, her eyes both gone astray
To watch yon am'rous couple in their play,
With bony and unkerchiefed neck defies
The rude inclemency of wintry skies,
And sails with lappethead and mincing airs,
Duly, at clink of bell, to morning prayers.[*]
To thrift and parsimony much inclined,
She yet allows herself that boy behind.
The shiv'ring urchin, bending as he goes,
With slip-shod heels and dewdrop at his nose;
His predecessor's coat advanced to wear,
Which future pages yet are doomed to share,
Carries her Bible tucked beneath his arm,
And hides his hands to keep his fingers warm.

    She, half an angel in her own account,
Doubts not hereafter with the saints to mount,
Though not a grace appears, on strictest search,
But that she fasts, and, *item*, goes to church.
Conscious of age, she recollects her youth,
And tells, not always with an eye to truth,
Who spanned her waist, and who, where'er he came,
Scrawled upon glass Miss Bridget's lovely name;
Who stole her slipper, filled it with tokay,
And drank the little bumper ev'ry day.
Of temper as envenomed as an asp,
Censorious, and her ev'ry word a wasp;
In faithful memory she records the crimes,
Or real, or fictitious, of the times;
Laughs at the reputations she has torn,
And holds them, dangling at arm's length, in scorn.

    Such are the fruits of sanctimonious pride,
Of malice fed while flesh is mortified:

---

[*]    This and the following describe the print by William Hogarth "Morning," from his series *Times of the Day* (1738). She is here depicted as a "woman of the Pharisees."

Take, madam, the reward of all your pray'rs,
Where hermits and where Bramins meet with theirs;
Your portion is with them.—Nay, never frown;
But, if you please, some fathoms lower down.

Artist, attend! your brushes and your paint—
Produce them—take a chair—now draw a saint.
Oh, sorrowful and sad! the streaming tears
Channel her cheeks—a Niobe appears!
Is this a saint? Throw tints and all away—
True piety is cheerful as the day;
Will weep indeed, and heave a pitying groan,
For others' woes, but smiles upon her own.

What purpose has the King of saints in view?
Why falls the gospel like a gracious dew?
To call up plenty from the teeming earth,
Or curse the desert with a tenfold dearth?
Is it that Adam's offspring may be saved
From servile fear, or be the more enslaved?
To loose the links that galled mankind before,
Or bind them faster on, and add still more?
The freeborn Christian has no chains to prove;
Or, if a chain, the golden one of love:
No fear attends to quench his glowing fires,
What fear he feels his gratitude inspires.
Shall he, for such deliv'rance, freely wrought,
Recompense ill? He trembles at the thought.
His Master's int'rest and his own combined
Prompt ev'ry movement of his heart and mind:
Thought, word, and deed, his liberty evince;
His freedom is the freedom of a prince.

Man's obligations infinite, of course
His life should prove that he perceives their force:
His utmost he can render is but small—
The principle and motive all in all.
You have two servants—Tom, an arch, sly rogue,

From top to toe the Geta* now in vogue,
Genteel in figure, easy in address,
Moves without noise, and swift as an express,
Reports a message with a pleasing grace,
Expert in all the duties of his place:
Say, on what hinge does his obedience move?
Has he a world of gratitude and love?
No, not a spark—'tis all mere sharper's play;
He likes your house, your housemaid, and your pay;
Reduce his wages, or get rid of her,
Tom quits you, with—Your most obedient, sir.
    The dinner served, Charles takes his usual stand,
Watches your eye, anticipates command;
Sighs, if perhaps your appetite should fail;
And, if he but suspects a frown, turns pale;
Consults all day your int'rest and your ease,
Richly rewarded if he can but please;
And, proud to make his firm attachment known,
To save your life would nobly risk his own.

    Now which stands highest in your serious thought?
Charles, without doubt, say you—and so he ought;
One act, that from a thankful heart proceeds,
Excels ten thousand mercenary deeds.

    Thus Heaven approves as honest and sincere,
The work of gen'rous love and filial fear;
But, with averted eyes, the omniscient Judge
Scorns the base hireling, and the slavish drudge.

    Where dwell these matchless saints?—old Curio cries.
E'en at your side, Sir, and before your eyes,
The favoured few—the enthusiasts you despise.
And, pleased at heart, because on holy ground,
Sometimes a canting hypocrite is found,
Reproach a people with his single fall,
And cast his filthy raiment at them all.

---

\*    Name of a roguish slave in the play by Roman playwright Terence, *Phormio*, who is nontheless obsequious in flattery and surface good manners.

Attend!—an apt similitude shall show
Whence springs the conduct that offends you so.

See where it smokes along the sounding plain,
Blown all aslant, a driving, dashing rain,
Peal upon peal redoubling all around,
Shakes it again, and faster to the ground;
Now flashing wide, now glancing as in play,
Swift beyond thought the lightnings dart away.
Ere yet it came, the traveler urged his steed,
And hurried, but with unsuccessful speed;
Now, drenched throughout, and hopeless of his case,
He drops the rein, and leaves him to his pace.
Suppose, unlooked for in a scene so rude,
Long hid by interposing hill or wood,
Some mansion, neat and elegantly dress'd,
By some kind hospitable heart possessed,
Offer him warmth, security, and rest;
Think with what pleasure, safe, and at his ease,
He hears the tempest howling in the trees;
What glowing thanks his lips and heart employ,
While danger past is turned to present joy.
So fares it with the sinner, when he feels
A growing dread of vengeance at his heels:
His conscience, like a glassy lake before,
Lashed into foaming waves, begins to roar;
The law, grown clamorous, though silent long,
Arraigns him—charges him with every wrong—
Asserts the right of his offended Lord;
And death, or restitution, is the word:
The last impossible, he fears the first,
And, having well deserved, expects the worst.
Then welcome refuge and a peaceful home;
O for a shelter from the wrath to come!*
Crush me, ye rocks; ye falling mountains, hide,†
Or bury me in ocean's angry tide!—
The scrutiny of those all-seeing eyes

---

*      Cf. Luke 3:7.
†      Luke 23:30; Revelation 6:16.

I dare not—And you need not, God replies;
The remedy you want I freely give;
The Book shall teach you—read, believe, and live!
'Tis done—the raging storm is heard no more,
Mercy receives him on her peaceful shore;
And Justice, guardian of the dread command,
Drops the red vengeance from his willing hand.
A soul redeem'd demands a life of praise;
Hence the complexion of his future days,
Hence a demeanour holy and unspeck'd,
And the world's hatred, as its sure effect.
    Some lead a life unblameable and just,
Their own dear virtue their unshaken trust:
They never sin—or, if (as all offend)
Some trivial slips their daily walk attend,
The poor are near at hand, the charge is small,
A slight gratuity atones for all!
For though the Pope has lost his int'rest here,
And pardons are not sold as once they were,
No Papist more desirous to compound,
Than some grave sinners upon English ground.
That plea refuted, other quirks they seek—
Mercy is infinite, and man is weak;
The future shall obliterate the past,
And heaven, no doubt, shall be their home at last.

    Come, then—a still, small whisper in your ear—
He has no hope who never had a fear;
And he that never doubted of his state,
He may, perhaps—perhaps he may—too late.

    The path to bliss abounds with many a snare;
Learning is one, and wit, however rare.
The Frenchman, first in literary fame,
(Mention him, if you please. Voltaire?—The same),*
With spirit, genius, eloquence, supplied,
Lived long, wrote much, laughed heartily, and died;

---

*      Voltaire (1694-1778), French philosopher and famous atheistical opponent of
Christianity, whose *La Henriade* had been partially translated by Cowper.

The Scripture was his jest-book, whence he drew
*Bon-mots* to gall the Christian and the Jew;
An infidel in health, but what when sick?
Oh—then a text would touch him at the quick.
View him at Paris in his last career,
Surrounding throngs the demi-god revere;
Exalted on his pedestal of pride,
And fumed with frankincense on ev'ry side,
He begs their flatt'ry with his latest breath;
And, smothered in't at last, is praised to death!

   Yon cottager, who weaves at her own door,
Pillow and bobbins all her little store;
Content, though mean; and cheerful, if not gay,
Shuffling her threads about the live-long day,
Just earns a scanty pittance; and at night
Lies down secure, her heart and pocket light:
She, for her humble sphere by nature fit,
Has little understanding, and no wit,
Receives no praise; but though her lot be such,
(Toilsome and indigent) she renders much;
Just knows, and knows no more, her Bible true—
A truth the brilliant Frenchman never knew;
And in that charter reads with sparkling eyes,
Her title to a treasure in the skies.

Oh, happy peasant! Oh, unhappy bard!
His the mere tinsel, her's the rich reward;
He praised, perhaps, for ages yet to come;
She never heard of half a mile from home;
He, lost in errors, his vain heart prefers;
She, safe in the simplicity of her's.

   Not many wise, rich, noble, or profound
In science, win one inch of heavenly ground.\*
And is it not a mortifying thought
The poor should gain it, and the rich should not?

---

\*    Luke 10:21; cf. 1 Cor. 1:19-20; 27.

No—the voluptuaries, who ne'er forget
One pleasure lost, lose heaven without regret;
Regret would rouse them, and give birth to prayer;
Prayer would add faith, and faith would fix them there.

Not that the Former of us all in this,
Or aught he does, is governed by caprice;
The supposition is replete with sin,
And bears the brand of blasphemy burnt in.
Not so—the silver trumpet's heavenly call
Sounds for the poor, but sounds alike for all:
Kings are invited; and, would kings obey,
No slaves on earth more welcome were than they;
But royalty, nobility, and state,
Are such a dead preponderating weight,
That endless bliss, (how strange soe'er it seem)
In counterpoise, flies up and kicks the beam.
'Tis open, and ye cannot enter—why?
Because ye will not, Conyers* would reply—
And he says much that many may dispute
And cavil at with ease, but none refute.
Oh, bless'd effect of penury and want,
The seed sown there, how vigorous is the plant!
No soil like poverty for growth divine,
As leanest land supplies the richest wine.
Earth gives too little, giving only bread,
To nourish pride, or turn the weakest head:
To them the sounding jargon of the schools
Seems what it is—a cap and bells for fools:
The light they walk by, kindled from above,
Shews them the shortest way to life and love:
They, strangers to the controversial field,
Where deists, always foiled, yet scorn to yield,
And never checked by what impedes the wise,
Believe, rush forward, and possess the prize.

---

* Conyers (1724-1786) prominent evangelical, vicar of St. Paul's, Deptford, who
urged John Newton to call upon Cowper in 1767, leading to the move to Olney, Newton's
parish.

Envy, ye great, the dull unlettered small:
Ye have much cause for envy—but not all.
We boast some rich ones whom the gospel sways;
And one who wears a coronet, and prays;*
Like gleanings of an olive-tree, they show
Here and there one upon the topmost bough.

How readily, upon the gospel plan
That question has its answer—What is man?
Sinful and weak, in ev'ry sense a wretch;
An instrument, whose chords, upon the stretch,
And strained to the last screw that he can bear,
Yield only discord in his Maker's ear;
Once the blest residence of truth divine,
Glorious as Solyma's interior shrine,†
Where, in his own oracular abode,
Dwelt visibly the light-creating God;
But made long since, like Babylon of old,
A den of mischiefs never to be told:
And she, once mistress of the realms around,
Now scattered wide, and nowhere to be found,
As soon shall rise and re-ascend the throne,
By native power and energy her own,
As nature, at her own peculiar cost,
Restore to man the glories he has lost.
Go—bid the winter cease to chill the year;
Replace the wandering comet in his sphere;
Then boast (but wait for that unhoped-for hour)
The self-restoring arm of human power.
But what is man in his own proud esteem?‡
Hear him—himself the poet and the theme:
A monarch clothed with majesty and awe,
His mind his kingdom, and his will his law;
Grace in his mien, and glory in his eyes,

---

* William Legge (1731-1801), second Earl of Dartmouth, schoolmate of Cowper
both at Westminster and Trinity College, Oxford, friend of the Countess of Huntingdon,
nominated John Newton to the curacy at Olney.
† Second component of the Greek for "Jerusalem."
‡ Ps 8:4-9; but this psalm underlies much of the entire poem.

Supreme on earth, and worthy of the skies,
Strength in his heart, dominion in his nod,
And, thunderbolts excepted, quite a God!

So sings he, charmed with his own mind and form,
The song magnificent—the theme a worm!
Himself so much the source of his delight,
His Maker has no beauty in his sight.
See where he sits, contemplative and fixed,
Pleasure and wonder in his features mixed;
His passions tamed, and all at his control,
How perfect the composure of his soul!
Complacency has breathed a gentle gale
O'er all his thoughts, and swelled his easy sail:
His books well trimmed, and in the gayest style,
Like regimented coxcombs, rank and file,
Adorn his intellects as well as shelves,
And teach him notions splendid as themselves:
The Bible only stands neglected there—
Though that of all most worthy of his care;

And, like an infant, troublesome awake,
Is left to sleep, for peace and quiet sake.

What shall the man deserve of human kind,
Whose happy skill and industry combined
Shall prove (what argument could never yet)
The Bible an imposture and a cheat?
The praises of the libertine professed,
The worst of men, and curses of the best.
Where should the living, weeping o'er his woes;
The dying, trembling at the awful close;
Where the betrayed, forsaken, and oppressed;
The thousands whom the world forbids to rest;
Where should they find (those comforts at an end
The Scripture yields), or hope to find, a friend?
Sorrow might muse herself to madness then;
And, seeking exile from the sight of men,
Bury herself in solitude profound,

Grow frantic with her pangs, and bite the ground.
Thus often unbelief, grown sick of life,
Flies to the tempting pool, or felon knife.
The jury meet, the coroner is short,
And lunacy the verdict of the court.
Reverse the sentence, let the truth be known,
Such lunacy is ignorance alone.
They knew not, what some bishops may not know,
That Scripture is the only cure of woe.
That field of promise how it flings abroad
Its odour o'er the Christian's thorny road!
The soul, reposing on assured relief,
Feels herself happy amidst all her grief,
Forgets her labour as she toils along,
Weeps tears of joy, and bursts into a song.

But the same word, that, like the polished share,
Ploughs up the roots of a believer's care,
Kills too the flow'ry weeds, where'er they grow,
That bind the sinner's Bacchanalian brow.
Oh, that unwelcome voice of heavenly love,
Sad messenger of mercy from above!
How does it grate upon his thankless ear,
Crippling his pleasures with the cramp of fear!
His will and judgment at continual strife,
That civil war embitters all his life;
In vain he points his pow'rs against the skies,
In vain he closes or averts his eyes,
Truth will intrude—she bids him yet beware;
And shakes the sceptic in the scorner's chair.*
Though various foes against the Truth combine,
Pride above all opposes her design;
Pride, of a growth superior to the rest,
The subtlest serpent, with the loftiest crest,
Swells at the thought, and, kindling into rage,
Would hiss the cherub Mercy from the stage.

*     Psalm 1:1—"the seat of the scornful."

And is the soul, indeed, so lost?—she cries;
Fallen from her glory, and too weak to rise?
Torpid and dull, beneath a frozen zone,
Has she no spark that may be deemed her own?
Grant her indebted to what zealots call
Grace undeserved—yet, surely, not for all!
Some beams of rectitude she yet displays,
Some love of virtue, and some pow'r to praise;
Can lift herself above corporeal things,
And, soaring on her own unborrowed wings,
Possess herself of all that's good or true,
Assert the skies, and vindicate her due.
Past indiscretion is a venial crime;
And if the youth, unmellowed yet by time,
Bore on his branch, luxuriant then and rude,
Fruits of a blighted size, austere and crude,
Maturer years shall happier stores produce,
And meliorate the well concocted juice.
Then, conscious of her meritorious zeal,
To justice she may make her bold appeal;
And leave to Mercy, with a tranquil mind,
The worthless and unfruitful of mankind,

Hear, then, how Mercy, slighted and defied,
Retorts the affront against the crown of pride.

Perish the virtue, as it ought, abhorred,
And the fool with it, who insults his Lord.
The atonement a Redeemer's love has wrought
Is not for you—the righteous need it not.[*]
Seest thou yon harlot, wooing all she meets,
The worn-out nuisance of the public streets;
Herself from morn to night, from night to morn,
Her own abhorrence, and as much your scorn!
The gracious show'r, unlimited and free,
Shall fall on her, when Heaven denies it thee.
Of all that wisdom dictates, this the drift—
That man is dead in sin, and life a gift.[†]

---

[*]    Cf. Matthew 9:13; Luke 5:32.
[†]    Luke 7

Is virtue, then, unless of Christian growth,
Mere fallacy, or foolishness, or both?
Ten thousand sages lost in endless woe,
For ignorance of what they could not know?
That speech betrays at once a bigot's tongue—
Charge not a God with such outrageous wrong!
Truly, not I—the partial light men have,
My creed persuades me, well employed, may save;
While he that scorns the noon-day beam, perverse,
Shall find the blessing, unimproved, a curse.
Let heathen worthies,* whose exalted mind
Left sensuality and dross behind,
Possess, for me, their undisputed lot,
And take, unenvied, the reward they sought:
But still in virtue of a Saviour's plea,
Not blind by choice, but destined not to see.
Their fortitude and wisdom were a flame
Celestial, though they knew not whence it came,
Derived from the same source of light and grace
That guides the Christian in his swifter race.
Their judge was conscience, and her rule their law;
That rule, pursued with reverence and with awe,
Led them, however falt'ring, faint, and slow,
From what they knew to what they wished to know.
But let not him that shares a brighter day
Traduce the splendour of a noon-tide ray,
Prefer the twilight of a darker time,
And deem his base stupidity no crime;
The wretch, who slights the bounty of the skies,
And sinks, while favoured with the means to rise,
Shall find them rated at their full amount,
The good he scorned all carried to account.

    Marshalling all his terrors as he came;
Thunder, and earthquake, and devouring flame;
From Sinai's top Jehovah gave the law—
Life for obedience—death for ev'ry flaw.

---

\*     The lines which follow reflect Romans 2, esp. 2:14-16.

When the great Sov'reign would his will express,
He gives a perfect rule; what can he less?
And guards it with a sanction as severe
As vengeance can inflict, or sinners fear:
Else his own glorious rights he would disclaim,
And man might safely trifle with his name.
He bids him glow with unremitting love
To all on earth, and to himself above;
Condemns the injurious deed, the sland'rous tongue,
The thought that meditates a brother's wrong:
Brings not alone the more conspicuous part—
His conduct—to the test, but tries his heart.

Hark! universal nature shook and groan'd,
'Twas the last trumpet—see the Judge enthroned:*
Rouse all your courage at your utmost need,
Now summon every virtue—stand, and plead.
What! silent? Is your boasting heard no more?
That self-renouncing wisdom, learn'd before,
Had shed immortal glories on your brow,
That all your virtues cannot purchase now.

All joy to the believer! He can speak—
Trembling, yet happy; confident, yet meek.

Since the dear hour that brought me to thy foot,
And cut up all my follies by the root,
I never trusted in an arm but thine,
Nor hoped, but in thy righteousness divine:
My pray'rs and alms, imperfect, and defiled,
Were but the feeble efforts of a child;
Howe'er perform'd, it was their brightest part
That they proceeded from a grateful heart:
Cleansed in thine own all purifying blood,
Forgive their evil, and accept their good:
I cast them at thy feet—my only plea
Is what it was—dependence upon thee:

---

*    Cf. 1 Corinthians 15:52; 1 Thessalonians 4:16.

While struggling in the vale of tears below,
That never fail'd, nor shall it fail me now.

Angelic gratulations rend the skies,
Pride falls unpitied, never more to rise,
Humility is crowned; and Faith receives the prize.

# HOPE (1781)

*Doceas iter, et sacra ostia pandas.—Virg. Aen. 6.*

Ask what is human life—the sage replies,
With disappointment low'ring in his eyes,
A painful passage o'er a restless flood,
A vain pursuit of fugitive false good,
A scene of fancied bliss and heart-felt care,
Closing at last in darkness and despair.
The poor, inured to drudg'ry and distress,
Act without aim, think little, and feel less,
And no where, but in feigned Arcadian scenes,
Taste happiness, or know what pleasure means.
Riches are pass'd away from hand to hand,
As fortune, vice, or folly, may command.
As in a dance the pair that take the lead
Turn downward, and the lowest pair succeed,
So shifting and so various is the plan
By which Heaven rules the mix't affairs of man:
Vicissitude wheels round the motley crowd,
The rich grow poor, the poor become purse-proud;
Bus'ness is labour, and man's weakness such,
Pleasure is labour too, and tires us much,
The very sense of it foregoes its use,
By repetition palled, by age obtuse.
Youth lost in dissipation, we deplore,
Through life's sad remnant, what no sighs restore;
Our years, a fruitless race without a prize,
Too many, yet too few to make us wise.

Dangling his cane about, and taking snuff,
Lothario* cries, What philosophic stuff—
O querulous and weak!—whose useless brain
Once thought of nothing, and now thinks in vain;
Whose eye, reverted, weeps o'er all the past,
Whose prospect shews thee a disheart'ning waste;
Would age in thee resign his wintry reign,
And youth invigorate that frame again,
Renew'd desire would grace with other speech
Joys always prized—when placed within our reach.

For lift thy palsied head, shake off the gloom
That overhangs the borders of thy tomb,
See nature, gay, as when she first began;
With smiles alluring her admirer man;
She spreads the morning over eastern hills,
Earth glitters with the drops the night distils;
The sun, obedient, at her call appears
To fling his glories o'er the robe she wears;
Banks clothed with flowers, groves filled with sprightly
        sounds,
The yellow tilth, green meads, rocks, rising grounds,
Streams edged with osiers, fatt'ning ev'ry field
Where'er they flow, now seen and now conceal'd;
From the blue rim where skies and mountains meet,
Down to the very turf beneath thy feet,
Ten thousand charms, that only fools despise,
Or pride can look at with indiff'rent eyes,
All speak one language, all with one sweet voice
Cry to her universal realm, Rejoice!
Man feels the spur of passions and desires,
And she gives largely more than he requires;
Not that, his hours devoted all to care,
Hollow-eyed abstinence, and lean despair,
The wretch may pine, while to his smell, taste, sight,
She holds a paradise of rich delight;
But gently to rebuke his awkward fear,

---

*    Lothario is the name of the rake who seduced the heroine in Nicholas Rowe's *The Fair Penitent* (1703), and it quickly became eponymous for such a character generally.

To prove that what she gives she gives sincere,
To banish hesitation, and proclaim
His happiness her dear, her only aim.
'Tis grave philosophy's absurdest dream,
That Heaven's intentions are not what they seem,
That only shadows are dispensed below,
And earth has no reality but woe.

Thus things terrestrial wear a diff'rent hue,
As youth or age persuades; and neither true:
So, Flora's wreath through coloured crystal seen,
The rose or lily appears blue or green,
But still the imputed tints are those alone
The medium represents, and not their own.

To rise at noon, sit slipshod and undressed,
To read the news, or fiddle, as seems best,
Till half the world comes rattling at his door,
To fill the dull vacuity till four;
And, just when evening turns the blue vault grey,
To spend two hours in dressing for the day;
To make the sun a bauble without use,
Save for the fruits his heavenly beams produce;
Quite to forget, or deem it worth no thought,
Who bids him shine, or if he shine or not;
Through mere necessity to close his eyes
Just when the larks and when the shepherds rise;
Is such a life, so tediously the same,
So void of all utility or aim,
That poor Jonquil,* with almost ev'ry breath,
Sighs for his exit, vulgarly called death:
For he, with all his follies, has a mind
Not yet so blank, or fashionably blind,
But now and then, perhaps, a feeble ray
Of distant wisdom shoots across his way,
By which he reads, that life without a plan,
As useless as the moment it began,

---

*    Floral name for an effete youth; today one might substitute "Pansy" for the same
effect.

Serves merely as a soil for discontent
To thrive in; an encumbrance ere half spent.
Oh! weariness beyond what asses feel,
That tread the circuit of the cistern wheel;
A dull rotation, never at a stay,
Yesterday's face twin image of to-day;
While conversation, an exhausted stock,
Grows drowsy as the clicking of a clock.
No need, he cries, of gravity stuffed out
With academic dignity devout,
To read wise lectures—vanity the text!
Proclaim the remedy, ye learned, next;
For truth, self-evident, with pomp impress'd,
Is vanity surpassing all the rest.

That remedy, not hid in deeps profound,
Yet seldom sought where only to be found,
While passion turns aside from its due scope
The inquirer's aim, that remedy is Hope.
Life is his gift, from whom whate'er life needs,
With every good and perfect gift,* proceeds;
Bestowed on man, like all that we partake,
Royally, freely, for his bounty' sake;
Transient indeed, as is the fleeting hour,
And yet the seed of an immortal flow'r;
Design'd, in honour of his endless love,
To fill with fragrance his abode above;
No trifle, howsoever short it seem,
And, howsoever shadowy, no dream;
Its value, what no thought can ascertain,
Nor all an angel's eloquence explain.

Men deal with life as children with their play,
Who first misuse, then cast their toys away;
Live to no sober purpose, and contend
That their Creator had no serious end.
When God and man stand opposite in view,

---

*    Cf. James 1:17.

Man's disappointment must of course ensue.
The just Creator condescends to write,
In beams of inextinguishable light,
His names of wisdom, goodness, pow'r, and love,
On all that blooms below, or shines above;
To catch the wand'ring notice of mankind,
And teach the world, if not perversely blind,
His gracious attributes, and prove the share
His offspring hold in his paternal care.
If, led from earthly things to things divine,*
His creature thwart not his august design,
Then praise is heard instead of reas'ning pride,
And captious cavil and complaint subside.
Nature, employed in her allotted place,
Is handmaid to the purposes of grace;
By good vouchsafed, makes known superior good,
And bliss not seen, by blessings understood:
That bliss, revealed in Scripture, with a glow
Bright as the covenant-insuring bow,
Fires all his feelings with a noble scorn
Of sensual evil, and thus Hope is born.

　　Hope sets the stamp of vanity on all
That men have deemed substantial since the fall,
Yet has the wondrous virtue to educe
From emptiness itself a real use;
And, while she takes, as at a father's hand,
What health and sober appetite demand,
From fading good derives, with chemic† art,
That lasting happiness, a thankful heart.
Hope, with uplifted foot, set free from earth,
Pants for the place of her ethereal birth,
On steady wings sails through the immense abyss,
Plucks amaranthine joys from bow'rs of bliss,
And crowns the soul, while yet a mourner here,
With wreaths like those triumphant spirits wear.

---

* 　　Cf. Romans 1:20.
† 　　i.e., "alchemical"

Hope, as an anchor firm and sure, holds fast*
The Christian vessel, and defies the blast.
Hope! nothing else can nourish and secure
His new-born virtues, and preserve him pure.
Hope! let the wretch, once conscious of the joy,
Whom now despairing agonies destroy,
Speak, for he can, and none so well as he,
What treasures centre, what delights, in thee.
Had he the gems, the spices, and the land
That boasts the treasure, all at his command;
The fragrant grove, the inestimable mine,
Were light, when weighed against one smile of thine.

Though clasp'd and cradled in his nurse's arms,
He shines with all a cherub's artless charms,
Man is the genuine offspring of revolt,
Stubborn and sturdy, a wild ass's colt;†
His passions, like the wat'ry stores that sleep
Beneath the smiling surface of the deep,
Wait but the lashes of a wintry storm,
To frown and roar, and shake his feeble form.
From infancy, through childhood's giddy maze,
Froward at school, and fretful in his plays,
The puny tyrant burns to subjugate
The free republic of the whip-gig state.
If one, his equal in athletic frame,
Or, more provoking still, of nobler name,
Dare step across his arbitrary views,
An Iliad, only not in verse, ensues:
The little Greeks look trembling at the scales,
Till the best tongue, or heaviest hand, prevails.

Now see him launch'd into the world at large:
If priest, supinely droning o'er his charge,
Their fleece his pillow, and his weekly drawl,
Though short, too long, the price he pays for all.
If lawyer, loud whatever cause he plead,

---

*    Hebrews 6:19.
†    Cf. Job 11:12.

49

But proudest of the worst, if that succeed;
Perhaps a grave physician, gathering fees,
Punctu'lly paid for length'ning out disease;
No COTTON,* whose humanity sheds rays,
That make superior skill his second praise;
If arms engage him, he devotes to sport
His date of life, so likely to be short;
A soldier may be anything, if brave;
So may a tradesman, if not quite a knave.
Such stuff the world is made of; and mankind,
To passion, int'rest, pleasure, whim, resign'd,
Insist on, as if each were his own pope,
Forgiveness, and the privilege of hope.
But conscience, in some awful silent hour,
When captivating lusts have lost their pow'r—
Perhaps when sickness, or some fearful dream,
Reminds him of religion, hated theme—
Starts from the down, on which she lately slept,
And tells of laws despised, at least not kept;
Shows, with a pointing finger, but no noise,
A pale procession of past sinful joys,
All witnesses of blessings foully scorned,
And life abused, and not to be suborned.
Mark these, she says; these, summoned from afar,
Begin their march to meet thee at the bar;
There find a Judge inexorably just,
And perish there, as all presumption must.

Peace be to those (such peace as earth can give)
Who live in pleasure, dead e'en while they live;†
Born capable indeed of heav'nly truth;
But down to latest age, from earliest youth,
Their mind a wilderness, through want of care,
The plough of wisdom never ent'ring there.
Peace (if insensibility may claim

---

\*    Dr. Nathaniel Cotton (1705-88), Cowper's attending physician while he has
hospitalized at St. Albans (1763-65), specialized in mental illness. He was himself a
minor poet and an evangelist.
†    1 Timothy 5:6.

A right to the meek honours of her name)
To men of pedigree, their noble race
Emulous always of the nearest place
To any throne except the throne of grace.
(Let cottagers and unenlightened swains
Revere the laws they dream that Heaven ordains;
Resort on Sundays to the house of prayer,
And ask, and fancy they find, blessings there.)
Themselves, perhaps, when weary they retreat
T'enjoy cool nature in a country seat,
T'exchange the centre of a thousand trades,
For clumps, and lawns, and temples, and cascades,
May now and then their velvet cushions take.
And seem to pray, for good example sake;
Judging, in charity, no doubt, the town
Pious enough, and having need of none.
Kind souls! to teach their tenantry to prize
What they themselves, without remorse, despise:
Nor hope have they, nor fear, of aught to come—
As well for them had prophecy been dumb.
They could have held the conduct they pursue,
Had Paul of Tarsus lived and died a Jew;
And truth, proposed to reas'ners wise as they,
Is a pearl cast—completely cast away.

   They die.—Death lends them, pleased, and as in sport,
All the grim honours of his ghastly court.
Far other paintings grace the chamber now,
Where late we saw the mimic landscape glow:
The busy heralds hang the sable scene
With mournful 'scutcheons, and dim lamps between;
Proclaim their titles to the crowd around,
But they that wore them move not at the sound;
The coronet, placed idly at their head,
Adds nothing now to the degraded dead;
And ev'n the star that glitters on the bier
Can only say—Nobility lies here.
Peace to all such—'twere pity to offend,
By useless censure, whom we cannot mend;

Life without hope can close but in despair—
'Twas there we found them, and must leave them there.
   As, when two pilgrims in a forest stray,
Both may be lost, yet each in his own way;
So fares it with the multitudes beguiled
In vain opinion's waste and dang'rous wild;
Ten thousand rove the brakes and thorns among,
Some eastward, and some westward, and all wrong.
But here, alas! the fatal diff'rence lies,
Each man's belief is right in his own eyes;*
And he that blames what they have blindly chose,
Incurs resentment for the love he shews.

   Say, botanist, within whose province fall
The cedar and the hyssop on the wall,†
Of all that deck the lanes, the fields, the bowers,
What parts the kindred tribes of weeds and flowers?
Sweet scent, or lovely form, or both combined,
Distinguish ev'ry cultivated kind;
The want of both denotes a meaner breed,
And Chloe from her garland picks the weed.
Thus hopes of every sort, whatever sect
Esteem them, sow them, rear them, and protect,
If wild in nature, and not duly found,
Gethsemane' in thy dear hallow'd ground,
That cannot bear the blaze of Scripture light,
Nor cheer the spirit, nor refresh the sight,
Nor animate the soul to Christian deeds,
(Oh cast them from thee!) are weeds, arrant weeds.

   Ethelred's† house, the centre of six ways,
Diverging each from each, like equal rays,
Himself as bountiful as April rains,

---

*     Proverbs 21:2.

†     1 Kings 4:33 lists these topics as amongst the subjects of Solomon's poetry and wise sayings.

‡     Anglo Saxon "Ethelred" means "wise lord" (*aethel* = lord; *red/rad* = counsel/ learned) here seems to refer backward to Solomon, but as a type for Christ. Thus, Matthew 22:1-14 is suggested by what follows, namely a recollection of the parable of the wedding feast, which Cowper reads as a parable about the character of grace.

Lord paramount of the surrounding plains,
Would give relief of bed and board to none,
But guests that sought it in th'appointed One;
And they might enter at his open door,

Ev'n till his spacious hall would hold no more.
He sent a servant forth by every road,
To sound his horn and publish it abroad,
That all might mark—knight, menial, high, and low—
An ordinance it concerned them much to know.
If, after all, some headstrong, hardy lout
Would disobey, though sure to be shut out,
Could he with reason murmur at his case,
Himself sole author of his own disgrace?
No! the decree was just and without flaw;
And he that made, had right to make, the law;
His sov'reign pow'r and pleasure unrestrained,
The wrong was his who wrongfully complained.

Yet half mankind maintain a churlish strife
With him the Donor of eternal life,
Because the deed, by which his love confirms
The largess he bestows, prescribes the terms.
Compliance with his will your lot insures—
Accept it only, and the boon is yours.
And sure it is as kind to smile and give,
As with a frown to say: Do this, and live!
Love is not pedlar's trump'ry, bought and sold;
He *will* give freely, or he *will* withhold;
His soul abhors a mercenary thought,
And him as deeply who abhors it not;
He stipulates indeed, but merely this—
That man will freely take an unbought bliss,
Will trust him for a faithful, gen'rous part,
Nor set a price upon a willing heart.
Of all the ways that seem to promise fair,
To place you where his saints his presence share,
This only can; for this plain cause, expressed
In terms as plain—himself has shut the rest.

But oh the strife, the bick'ring, and debate,
The tidings of unpurchased heaven create!
The flirted fan, the bridle, and the toss,
All speakers, yet all language at a loss.
From stuccoed walls smart arguments rebound;
And beaus, adepts in every thing profound,
Die of disdain, or whistle off the sound.
Such is the clamour of rooks, daws, and kites,
Th'explosion of the levelled tube excites.
Where mould'ring abbey walls o'erhang the glade,
And oaks coeval spread a mournful shade.
The screaming nations, hov'ring in mid air,
Loudly resent the stranger's freedom there,
And seem to warn him never to repeat
His bold intrusion on their dark retreat.

   Adieu, Vinosa* cries, ere yet he sips
The purple bumper, trembling at his lips,
Adieu to all morality—if grace
Make works a vain ingredient in the case!
The Christian hope is—Waiter, draw the cork—
If I mistake not—Blockhead! with a fork—
Without good works, whatever some may boast,
Mere folly and delusion—Sir, your toast!—
My firm persuasion is, at least sometimes,
That Heaven will weigh man's virtues and his crimes
With nice attention, in a righteous scale,
And save or damn as these or those prevail.
I plant my foot upon this ground of trust,
And silence ev'ry fear with—God is just.
But if perchance, on some dull drizzling day,
A thought intrude that says, or seems to say,
If thus th'important cause is to be tried,
Suppose the beam should dip on the wrong side;

---

\*    *Vinosa:* here one who anaesthetizes himself by wine, oblivious to the true
character of grace, thus thinking of the Calvinistic view, in its relegation of good works
(or merit) as an invitation to anti-nomianism, or lawlessness. Cowper here suggests
that theological arguments about grace and worth tend to be unreflective exchanges of
clouded opinion.

I soon recover from these needless frights,
And, God is merciful—sets all to rights.
Thus, between justice, as my prime support,
And mercy, fled to as the last resort,
I glide and steal along with heaven in view,
And—pardon me—the bottle stands with you.

I never will believe, the colonel cries,
The sanguinary schemes that some devise,
Who make the good Creator, on their plan,
A being of less equity than man.
If appetite, or what divines call lust,
Which men comply with, e'en because they must,
Be punished with perdition, who is pure?
Then theirs, no doubt, as well as mine, is sure.
If sentence of eternal pain belong
To ev'ry sudden slip and transient wrong,
Then Heaven enjoins the fallible and frail
A hopeless task, and damns them if they fail—
My creed (whatever some creed-makers mean
By Athanasian nonsense, or Nicene)
My creed is—he is safe that does his best,
And death's a doom sufficient for the rest.

Right, says an ensign; and, for aught I see,
Your faith and mine substantially agree;
The best of every man's performance here
Is to discharge the duties of his sphere.
A lawyer's dealings should be just and fair,
Honesty shines with great advantage there.
Fasting and prayer sit well upon a priest—
A decent caution and reserve at least.
A soldier's best is courage in the field,
With nothing here that wants to be concealed;
Manly deportment, gallant, easy, gay;
A hand as lib'ral as the light of day.
The soldier thus endowed, who never shrinks,
Nor closets up his thoughts, whate'er he thinks,
Who scorns to do an injury by stealth,

Must go to heaven—and I must drink his health.
Sir Smug, he cries (for lowest at the board—
Just made fifth chaplain of his patron lord,
His shoulders witnessing by many a shrug
How much his feelings suffered—sat Sir Smug),
Your office is to winnow false from true;
Come, prophet, drink, and tell us—What think you?

   Sighing and smiling as he takes his glass,
Which they that woo preferment rarely pass,
Fallible man, the church-bred youth replies,
Is still found fallible, however wise;
And diff'ring judgments serve but to declare,
That truth lies somewhere, if we knew but where.
Of all it ever was my lot to read,
Of critics now alive or long since dead,
The book of all the world that charmed me most
Was—well-a-day, the title-page was lost!
The writer well remarks, a heart that knows
To take with gratitude what Heaven bestows,
With prudence always ready at our call,
To guide our use of it, is all in all.
Doubtless it is—To which, of my own store,
I superadd a few essentials more;
But these, excuse the liberty I take,
I wave just now, for conversation sake—
Spoke like an oracle, they all exclaim,
And add Right Rev'rend to Smug's honoured name.

   And yet our lot is given us in a land
Where busy arts are never at a stand;
Where science points her telescopic eye,
Familiar with the wonders of the sky;
Where bold inquiry, diving out of sight,
Brings many a precious pearl of truth to light;
Where nought eludes the persevering quest,
That fashion, taste, or luxury, suggest.

   But, above all, in her own light arrayed,

See Mercy's grand apocalypse displayed!
The sacred book no longer suffers wrong,
Bound in the fetters of an unknown tongue;
But speaks with plainness art could never mend,
What simplest minds can soonest comprehend.*
God gives the word—the preachers throng around,
Live from his lips, and spread the glorious sound:
That sound bespeaks salvation on her way,
The trumpet of a life-restoring day!
'Tis heard where England's eastern glory shines,
And in the gulfs of her Cornubian mines.†
And still it spreads. See Germany send forth
Her sons to pour it on the farthest north:
Fired with a zeal peculiar, they defy
The rage and rigour of a polar sky,
And plant successfully sweet Sharon's rose
On icy plains, and in eternal snows.

Oh blest within the inclosure of your rocks,
Not herds have ye to boast, nor bleating flocks;
Nor fertilizing streams your fields divide,
That shew, reversed, the villas on their side;
No groves have ye; no cheerful sound of bird,
Or voice of turtle, in your land is heard;
Nor grateful eglantine regales the smell
Of those that walk at ev'ning where ye dwell;
But winter, armed with terrors here unknown,
Sits absolute on his unshaken throne;
Piles up his stores amidst the frozen waste,
And bids the mountains he has built stand fast;
Beckons the legions of his storms away
From happier scenes, to make your land a prey;
Proclaims the soil a conquest he has won,
And scorns to share it with the distant sun.
—Yet truth is yours, remote, unenvied isle!
And peace, the genuine offspring of her smile;

---

\*     i.e., the Bible is available now in English translation, which each person can read for themself.

†     Reference to John Wesley's successful preaching in Cornwall.

The pride of letter'd ignorance, that binds
In chains of error our accomplish'd minds,
That decks, with all the splendour of the true,
A false religion, is unknown to you.
Nature indeed vouchsafes, for our delight,
The sweet vicissitudes of day and night:
Soft airs and genial moisture feed and cheer
Field, fruit, and flow'r, and ev'ry creature here;
But brighter beams, than his who fires the skies
Have risen at length on your admiring eyes,
That shoot into your darkest caves the day,
From which our nicer optics turn away.

Here see th'encouragement grace gives to vice,
The dire effect of mercy without price!
What were they? what some fools are made by art,
They were by nature—atheists, head and heart.
The gross idolatry blind heathens teach
Was too refined for them, beyond their reach.
Not e'en the glorious sun—though men revere
The monarch most that seldom will appear,
And though his beams, that quicken where they shine,
May claim some right to be esteemed divine—
Not e'en the sun, desirable as rare,
Could bend one knee, engage one votary there!
They were, what base credulity believes
True Christians are, dissemblers, drunkards, thieves.
The full-gorged savage, at his nauseous feast
Spent half the darkness, and snored out the rest,
Was one whom justice, on an equal plan,
Denouncing death upon the sins of man,
Might almost have indulged with an escape,
Chargeable only with a human shape.

What are they now?—Morality may spare
Her grave concern, her kind suspicions there:
The wretch who once sang wildly, danced, and laughed,
And sucked in dizzy madness with his draught,
Has wept a silent flood, reversed his ways,

Is sober, meek, benevolent, and prays,
Feeds sparingly, communicates his store,
Abhors the craft he boasted of before—
And he that stole has learned to steal no more.
Well spake the prophet, Let the desert sing,
Where sprang the thorn the spiry fir shall spring,*
And where unsightly and rank thistles grew,
Shall grow the myrtle and luxuriant yew.

Go now, and with important tone demand
On what foundation virtue is to stand,
If self-exalting claims be turn'd adrift,
And grace be grace indeed, and life a gift;
The poor reclaim'd inhabitant, his eyes
Glist'ning at once with pity and surprise,
Amazed that shadows should obscure the sight
Of one whose birth was in a land of light,
Shall answer, Hope, sweet Hope, has set me free,
And made all pleasures else mere dross to me.

These, amidst scenes as waste as if denied
The common care that waits on all beside,
Wild as if nature there, void of all good,
Play'd only gambols in a frantic mood,
(Yet charge not heavenly skill with having planned
A play-thing world, unworthy of his hand!)
Can see his love, though secret evil lurks
In all we touch, stamped plainly on his works;
Deem life a blessing with its numerous woes,
Nor spurn away a gift a God bestows.

Hard task, indeed, o'er arctic seas to roam!
Is hope exotic? grows it not at home?
Yes, but an object, bright as orient morn,
May press the eye too closely to be borne;
A distant virtue we can all confess,
It hurts our pride, and moves our envy, less.
Leuconomus (beneath well-sounding Greek

---

\*     Isaiah 35:11.

I slur a name a poet must not speak)*
Stood pilloried on infamy's high stage,
And bore the pelting scorn of half an age;
The very butt of slander, and the blot
For ev'ry dart that malice ever shot.
The man that mentioned *him* at once dismissed
All mercy from his lips, and sneered and hissed;
His crimes were such as Sodom never knew,
And perjury stood up to swear all true;
His aim was mischief, and his zeal pretence,
His speech rebellion against common sense;
A knave, when tried on honesty's plain rule;
And, when by that of reason, a mere fool;
The world's best comfort was, his doom was pass'd;
Die when he might, he must be damned at last.

    Now, Truth, perform thine office; waft aside
The curtain drawn by prejudice and pride,
Reveal (the man is dead) to wond'ring eyes
This more than monster in his proper guise.

    He loved the world that hated him: the tear
That dropped upon his Bible was sincere;
Assailed by scandal and the tongue of strife,
His only answer was a blameless life;
And he that forged, and he that threw, the dart,
Had each a brother's int'rest in his heart!
Paul's love of Christ, and steadiness unbribed,
Were copied close in him, and well transcribed.
He followed Paul—his zeal a kindred flame,
His apostolic charity the same.
Like him, cross'd cheerfully tempestuous seas,
Forsaking country, kindred, friends, and ease;
Like him he labour'd, and, like him, content
To bear, it, suffered shame where'er he went.

---

*      Greek *leuko* = white; *nomos* = "field": hence the Methodist but Calvinistic preacher, George Whitefield (1714-70). Here Cowper repeats the calumnies most often arrayed against him by secularist and broad-church writers in order to set set a stage for his subsquent defence of Whitefield.

Blush, calumny! and write upon his tomb,
If honest eulogy can spare thee room,
Thy deep repentance of thy thousand lies,
Which, aimed at him, have pierced th'offended skies;
And say, Blot out my sin, confessed, deplored,
Against thine image in thy saint, O Lord!

No blinder bigot, I maintain it still,
Than he who must have pleasure, come what will;
He laughs, whatever weapon Truth may draw,
And deems her sharp artillery mere straw.
Scripture, indeed, is plain; but God and he,
On Scripture ground are sure to disagree;
Some wiser rule must teach him how to live,
Than this his Maker has seen fit to give;
Supple and flexible as Indian cane,
To take the bend his appetites ordain;
Contrived to suit frail nature's crazy case,
And reconcile his lusts with saving grace.
By this, with nice precision of design,
He draws upon life's map a zig-zag line,
That shews how far 'tis safe to follow sin,
And where his danger and God's wrath begin.
By this he forms, as pleased he sports along,
His well-poised estimate of right and wrong;
And finds the modish manners of the day,
Though loose, as harmless as an infant's play.

Build by whatever plan caprice decrees,
With what materials, on what ground you please;
Your hope shall stand unblamed, perhaps admired,
If not that hope the Scripture has required.
The strange conceits, vain projects, and wild dreams,
With which hypocrisy for ever teems,
(Though other follies strike the public eye,
And raise a laugh) pass unmolested by;
But if, unblameable in word and thought,
A *man* arise—a man whom God has taught,

With all Elijah's dignity of tone,[*]
And all the love of the beloved John[†]—
To storm the citadels they build in air,
And smite th'untempered wall, 'tis death to spare.
To sweep away all refuges of lies,
And place, instead of quirks themselves devise,
*Lama sabachthani* before their eyes;[‡]
To prove that without Christ all gain is loss,[§]
All hope despair, that stands not on his cross;
Except the few his God may have impressed,
A tenfold frenzy seizes all the rest.

  Throughout mankind, the Christian kind at least,
There dwells a consciousness in ev'ry breast,
That folly ends where genuine hope begins,
And he that finds his heaven must lose his sins.
Nature opposes, with her utmost force,
This riving stroke, this ultimate divorce,[¶]
And, while Religion seems to be her view,
Hates with a deep sincerity *the true:*
For this—of all that ever influenced man,
Since Abel worshipp'd,[**] or the world began—
This only spares no lust; admits no plea;
But makes him, if at all, completely free;
Sounds forth the signal, as she mounts her car,
Of an eternal, universal war;
Rejects all treaty; penetrates all wiles;
Scorns with the same indiff'rence frowns and smiles;
Drives through the realms of sin, where riot reels,
And grinds his crown beneath her burning wheels!
Hence all that is in man—pride, passion, art,
Pow'rs of the mind, and feelings of the heart—

---

[*]    Luke 1:17.
[†]    Cf. John 13:23.
[‡]    Cf. Matthew 27:46.
[§]    Philippians 3:7; cf. Philippians 1:21.
[¶]    Cf. the title by C.S. Lewis, *The Great Divorce*, in which similar theological conversations take place.
[**]    Genesis 4:16.

62

Insensible of Truth's almighty charms,
Starts at her first approach, and sounds, To arms!
While Bigotry, with well-dissembled fears,
His eyes shut fast, his fingers in his ears,
Mighty to parry and push by God's Word
With senseless noise, his argument the sword,
Pretends a zeal for godliness and grace,
And spits abhorrence in the Christian's face.

    Parent of Hope, immortal Truth! make known
Thy deathless wreaths and triumphs, all thine own:
The silent progress of thy pow'r is such,
Thy means so feeble, and despised so much,
That few believe the wonders thou hast wrought,
And none can teach them but whom thou hast taught.
Oh, see me sworn to serve thee, and command
A painter's skill into a poet's hand!
That, while I, trembling, trace a work divine,
Fancy may stand aloof from the design,
And light, and shade, and ev'ry stroke, be thine.

    If ever thou hast felt another's pain,
If ever when he sighed hast sighed again,
If ever on thine eyelid stood the tear
That pity had engendered, drop one here!
This man was happy—had the world's good word,
And with it every joy it can afford;
Friendship and love seem'd tenderly at strife,
Which most should sweeten his untroubled life;
Politely learned, and of a gentle race,
Good-breeding and good sense gave all a grace,
And, whether at the toilette of the fair
He laughed and trifled, made him welcome there,
Or, if in masculine debate he shared,
Ensured him mute attention and regard.
Alas, how changed!—Expressive of his mind,
His eyes are sunk, arms folded, head reclined;
Those awful syllables, hell, death, and sin,
Though whispered, plainly tell what works within;

That conscience there performs her proper part,
And writes a doomsday sentence on his heart!
Forsaking, and forsaken of all friends,
He now perceives where earthly pleasure ends;
Hard task—for one who lately knew no care,
And harder still, as learnt beneath despair!
His hours no longer pass unmarked away,
A dark importance saddens every day;
He hears the notice of the clock, perplexed,
And cries—perhaps eternity strikes next!
Sweet music is no longer music here,
And laughter sounds like madness in his ear:
His grief the world of all her pow'r disarms;
Wine has no taste, and beauty has no charms:
God's holy Word, once trivial in his view,
Now by the voice of his experience true,
Seems, as it is, the fountain whence alone
Must spring that hope he pants to make his own.

Now let the bright reverse be known abroad;
Say man's a worm, and pow'r belongs to God.

As when a felon, whom his country's laws
Have justly doom'd for some atrocious cause,
Expects, in darkness and heart-chilling fears,
The shameful close of all his mispent years;
If chance, on heavy pinions slowly borne,
A tempest usher in the dreaded morn,
Upon his dungeon walls the lightning play,
The thunder seems to summon him away,
The warder at the door his key applies,
Shoots back the bolt, and all his courage dies:
If then, just then, all thoughts of mercy lost,
When Hope, long ling'ring, at last yields the ghost,
The sound of pardon pierce his startled ear,
He drops at once his fetters and his fear;
A transport glows in all he looks and speaks,
And the first thankful tears bedew his cheeks.
Joy, far superior joy, that much outweighs

The comfort of a few poor added days,
Invades, possesses, and o'erwhelms, the soul
Of him, whom Hope has with a touch made whole.*
'Tis heaven, all heaven, descending on the wings
Of the glad legions of the King of kings;
'Tis more—'tis God diffused through ev'ry part,
'Tis God himself triumphant in his heart!
Oh welcome now the sun's once hated light,
His noon-day beams were never half so bright.
Not kindred minds alone are call'd t'employ
Their hours, their days, in list'ning to his joy;
Unconscious nature, all that he surveys,
Rocks, groves, and streams must join him in his praise.

These are thy glorious works, eternal Truth,
The scoff of wither'd age and beardless youth;
These move the censure and the illib'ral grin
Of fools that hate thee and delight in sin:
But these shall last when night has quenched the pole,
And heaven is all departed as a scroll:†
And when, as justice has long since decreed,
This earth shall blaze, and a new world succeed,
Then these thy glorious works, and they who share
That hope which can alone exclude despair,
Shall live exempt from weakness and decay,
The brightest wonders of an endless day.‡

Happy the bard (if that fair name belong
To him that blends no fable with his song)§
Whose lines, uniting, by an honest art,
The faithful monitor's and poet's part,
Seek to delight, that they may mend mankind,
And, while they captivate, inform the mind:

---

* Cowper's sense of grace as unaccountable gift, a joy that surprises absolutely the
soul in despair, anticipates Wordsworth in his *Prelude* and C.S. Lewis, *Surprised by Joy*.

† Revelation 6:14.

‡ Here the sense of surprise experienced in grace anticipates the *parousia*, the final,
definitive surprise which is to conclude the master drama of human salvation. Cf. 2 Peter
3:10 ff.

§ Cf. Timothy 1:4.

Still happier, if he till a thankful soil,
And fruit reward his honourable toil:
But happier far, who comfort those that wait
To hear plain truth at Judah's hallowed gate:
Their language simple, as their manners meek,
No shining ornaments have they to seek;
Nor labour they, nor time, nor talents, waste,
In sorting flow'rs to suit a fickle taste;
But, while they speak the wisdom of the skies,
Which art can only darken and disguise,
The abundant harvest, recompence divine,
Repays their work—the gleaning only mine.

# CHARITY (1781)

*Quo nihil majus meliusve terris*
*Fata donavêre, bonique divi;*

*Nec dabunt, quamvis redeant in aurum*
*Tempora priscum.*
*—Hor. Lib. iv. Ode 2.*

Fairest and foremost of the train, that wait
On man's most dignified and happiest state,
Whether we name thee Charity or Love,
Chief grace below, and all in all above,
Prosper (I press thee with a pow'rful plea)
A task I venture on, impelled by thee:
Oh, never seen but in thy blest effects,
Or felt but in the soul that Heaven selects;
Who seeks to praise thee, and to make thee known
To other hearts, must have thee in his own.
Come, prompt me with benevolent desires,
Teach me to kindle at thy gentle fires,
And, though disgraced and slighted, to redeem
A poet's name, by making thee the theme.

God, working ever on a social plan,
By various ties attaches man to man:
He made at first, though free and unconfined,
One man the common father of the kind;
That every tribe, though placed as he sees best,
Where seas or deserts part them from the rest,
Diff'ring in language, manners, or in face,
Might feel themselves allied to all the race.
When Cook*—lamented, and with tears as just
As ever mingled with heroic dust—
Steered Britain's oak† into a world unknown,
And in his country's glory sought his own,
Wherever he found man to nature true,
The rights of man were sacred in his view.
He soothed with gifts, and greeted with a smile,
The simple native of the new-found isle;
He spurned the wretch that slighted or withstood
The tender argument of kindred blood,
Nor would endure that any should control
His free-born brethren of the southern pole.

But, though some nobler minds a law respect,
That none shall with impunity neglect,
In baser souls unnumbered evils meet,
To thwart its influence, and its end defeat.
While Cook is loved for savage lives he saved,
See Cortez‡ odious for a world enslaved!
Where wast thou then, sweet Charity? where then,
Thou tutelary friend of helpless men?
Wast thou in monkish cells and nunn'ries found,
Or building hospitals on English ground?
No.—Mammon makes the world his legatee
Through fear, not love; and Heaven abhors the fee.
Wherever found (and all men need thy care),

---

* Captain James Cook (1728-1779) explorer and amateur anthropologist, had been killed by natives of Hawaii but news of his death took until 1780 to reach England.

† i.e., oak-timbered ships.

‡ The Spanish explorer Hernando Cortés (1485-1547), by contrast with Cook a military conqueror of evil repute and savage methods, mostly in Mexico.

Nor age, nor infancy could find thee there.
The hand that slew till it could slay no more,
Was glued to the sword-hilt with Indian gore.
Their prince, as justly seated on his throne
As vain imperial Philip on his own,
Tricked out of all his royalty by art,
That stripped him bare, and broke his honest heart,
Died, by the sentence of a shaven priest,
For scorning what they taught him to detest.
How dark the veil that intercepts the blaze
Of Heaven's mysterious purposes and ways!
God stood not, though he seem'd to stand, aloof;
And at this hour the conqueror feels the proof:
The wreath he won drew down an instant curse,
The fretting plague* is in the public purse,
The cankered spoil corrodes the pining state,
Starved by that indolence their mines create.

Oh, could their ancient Incas rise again,
How would they take up Israel's taunting strain!
Art thou too fallen, Iberia? Do we see
The robber and the murd'rer weak as we?
Thou that hast wasted earth, and dared despise
Alike the wrath and mercy of the skies,
Thy pomp is in the grave, thy glory laid
Low in the pits thine avarice has made!†
We come with joy from our eternal rest.
To see th'oppressor in his turn oppressed.
Art thou the god, the thunder of whose hand
Rolled over all our desolated land,
Shook principalities and kingdoms down,
And made the mountains tremble at his frown?
The sword shall light upon thy boasted powers,
And waste them, as thy sword has wasted ours.‡
'Tis thus Omnipotence his law fulfils,
And vengeance executes what justice wills.

*     i.e., syphilis.
†     Possibly Isaiah 14:10-11.
‡     Cf. Matthew 26:52.

Again—the band of commerce was design'd
To associate all the branches of mankind;

And, if a boundless plenty be the robe,
Trade is the golden girdle of the globe.
Wise to promote whatever end he means,
God opens fruitful nature's various scenes:
Each climate needs what other climes produce,
And offers something to the gen'ral use;
No land but listens to the common call,
And in return receives supply from all.
This genial intercourse, and mutual aid,
Cheers what were else an universal shade,
Calls nature from her ivy-mantled den,
And softens human rock-work into men.
Ingenious Art, with her expressive face,
Steps forth to fashion and refine the race;
Not only fills necessity's demand,
But overcharges her capacious hand:
Capricious taste itself can crave no more
Than she supplies from her abounding store;
She strikes out all that luxury can ask,
And gains new vigour at her endless task.
Hers is the spacious arch, the shapely spire,
The painter's pencil, and the poet's lyre;
From her the canvas borrows light and shade,
And verse, more lasting, hues that never fade.
She guides the finger o'er the dancing keys,
Gives difficulty all the grace of ease,
And pours a torrent of sweet notes around
Fast as the thirsting ear can drink the sound.

These are the gifts of art; and art thrives most
Where commerce has enriched the busy coast;
He catches all improvements in his flight,
Spreads foreign wonders in his country's sight,
Imports what others have invented well,
And stirs his own to match them, or excel.
'Tis thus, reciprocating each with each,

Alternately the nations learn and teach;
While Providence enjoins to ev'ry soul
A union with the vast terraqueous whole.

   Heaven speed the canvas gallantly unfurl'd
To furnish and accommodate a world,
To give the pole the produce of the sun,
And knit the unsocial climates into one.
Soft airs and gentle heavings of the wave
Impel the fleet, whose errand is to save,
To succour wasted regions, and replace
The smile of opulence in sorrow's face.
Let nothing adverse, nothing unforeseen,
Impede the bark that ploughs the deep serene,
Charged with a freight transcending in its worth
The gems of India, nature's rarest birth,
That flies, like Gabriel on his Lord's commands,
A herald of God's love to pagan lands.
But, ah! what wish can prosper, or what prayer,
For merchants, rich in cargoes of despair,
Who drive a loathsome traffic, gauge, and span,
And buy the muscles and the bones of man?
The tender ties of father, husband, friend,
All bonds of nature, in that moment end;
And each endures, while yet he draws his breath,
A stroke as fatal as the scythe of death.
The sable warrior, frantic with regret
Of her he loves, and never can forget,
Loses in tears the far ereceding shore,
But not the thought that they must meet no more;
Deprived of her and freedom at a blow,
What has he left that he can yet forego?
Yes, to deep sadness sullenly resign'd,
He feels his body's bondage in his mind;
Puts off his generous nature, and to suit
His manners with his fate, puts on the brute.

   Oh, most degrading of all ills that wait
On man, a mourner in his best estate!

All other sorrows virtue may endure,
And find submission more than half a cure;
Grief is itself a med'cine, and bestowed
T'improve the fortitude that bears the load,
To teach the wand'rer, as his woes increase,
The path of wisdom, all whose paths are peace;*
But slavery!—Virtue dreads it as her grave:
Patience itself is meanness in a slave.
Or, if the will and sov'reignty of God
Bid suffer it a while, and kiss the rod,
Wait for the dawning of a brighter day,
And snap the chain the moment when you may.
Nature imprints upon whate'er we see,
That has a heart and life in it—Be free!
The beasts are chartered—neither age nor force
Can quell the love of freedom in a horse:
He breaks the cord that held him at the rack;
And, conscious of an unencumbered back,
Snuffs up the morning air, forgets the rein,
Loose fly his forelock and his ample mane;
Responsive to the distant neigh he neighs;
Nor stops, till, overleaping all delays,
He finds the pasture where his fellows graze.

Canst thou, and honoured with a Christian name,
Buy what is woman-born, and feel no shame?
Trade in the blood of innocence, and plead
Expedience as a warrant for the deed?
So may the wolf, whom famine has made bold
To quit the forest and invade the fold:
So may the ruffian, who with ghostly glide,
Dagger in hand, steals close to your bedside;
Not he, but his emergence forced the door,
He found it inconvenient to be poor.
Has God then given its sweetness to the cane—
Unless his laws be trampled on—in vain?
Built a brave world, which cannot yet subsist,

---

*     Cf. Proverbs 3:12.

Unless his right to rule it be dismissed?
Impudent blasphemy! So folly pleads,
And, avarice being judge, with ease succeeds.

But grant the plea—and let it stand for just,
That man make man his prey, because he *must*;
Still there is room for pity to abate,
And soothe the sorrows of so sad a state.
A Briton knows—or, if he knows it not,
The Scripture placed within his reach, he ought—
That souls have no discriminating hue,
Alike important in their Maker's view;*
That none are free from blemish since the fall,†
And love divine has paid one price for all.‡
The wretch that works and weeps without relief
Has One that notices his silent grief.
He, from whose hand alone all power proceeds,
Ranks its abuse among the foulest deeds,
Considers *all* injustice with a frown;
But *marks* the man that treads his fellow down.
Begone!—the whip and bell in that hard hand
Are hateful ensigns of usurped command.
Not Mexico could purchase kings a claim
To scourge him, weariness his only blame.
Remember, Heaven has an avenging rod,
To smite the poor is treason against God!§

Trouble is grudgingly and hardly brooked,
While life's sublimest joys are overlooked:
We wander o'er a sun-burnt thirsty soil,
Murm'ring and weary of our daily toil,
Forget t'enjoy the palm-tree's offered shade,
Or taste the fountain in the neighb'ring glade:
Else who would lose, that had the pow'r t'improve,
Th' occasion of transmuting fear to love?

---

*   Acts 10:34.
†   Romans 3:23; cf. 1 Corinthians 15:22.
‡   1 Corinthians 7:23
§   Cf. Ezekiel 18:12-13; Proverbs 14:31.

Oh, 'tis a godlike privilege to save!
And he that scorns it is himself a slave.
Inform his mind; one flash of heavenly day
Would heal his heart, and melt his chains away.
"Beauty for ashes" is a gift indeed!*
And slaves, by truth enlarged, are doubly freed.
Then would he say, submissive at thy feet,
While gratitude and love made service sweet,
My dear deliv'rer out of hopeless night,
Whose bounty bought me but to give me light,
I was a bondman on my native plain,
Sin forged, and ignorance made fast, the chain;
Thy lips have shed instruction as the dew,
Taught me what path to shun, and what pursue;
Farewell my former joys! I sigh no more
For Africa's once loved, benighted shore;
Serving a benefactor, I am free—
At my best home, if not exiled from thee.

Some men make gain a fountain whence proceeds
A stream of lib'ral and heroic deeds;
The swell of pity, not to be confined
Within the scanty limits of the mind,
Disdains the bank, and throws the golden sands,
A rich deposit, on the bord'ring lands:
These have an ear for his paternal call,
Who make some rich for the supply of all;
God's gift with pleasure in his praise employ;
And THORNTON† is familiar with the joy.

Oh, could I worship aught beneath the skies
That earth has seen, or fancy can devise,
Thine altar, sacred Liberty, should stand,
Built by no mercenary vulgar hand,
With fragrant turf, and flow'rs as wild and fair

*    Cf. Isaiah 61:3.
†    John Thorton (1720-90), wealthy merchant and benefactor of the poor and
supporter of the Evangelical movement. He sponsored the appointment to St. Mary
Woolnoth, in 1779, of John Newton.

As ever dressed a bank, or scented summer air!
Duly, as ever on the mountain's height
The peep of morning shed a dawning light,
Again, when evening in her sober vest
Drew the grey curtain of the fading west,
My soul should yield thee willing thanks and praise
For the chief blessings of my fairest days:
But that were sacrilege—praise is not thine,
But his who gave thee, and preserves thee mine:
Else I would say, and as I spake bid fly
A captive bird into the boundless sky,
This triple realm adores thee—thou art come
From Sparta hither, and art here at home.
We feel thy force still active, at this hour
Enjoy immunity from priestly power,
While conscience, happier than in ancient years,
Owns no superior but the God she fears.
Propitious spirit! yet expunge a wrong
Thy rights have suffered, and our land, too long.
Teach mercy to ten thousand hearts, that share
The fears and hopes of a commercial care.
Prisons expect the wicked, and were built
To bind the lawless, and to punish guilt;
But shipwreck, earthquake, battle, fire, and flood,
Are mighty mischiefs, not to be withstood;
And honest merit stands on slipp'ry ground,
Where covert guile and artifice abound.
Let just restraint, for public peace design'd,
Chain up the wolves and tigers of mankind;
The foe of virtue has no claim to thee—
But let insolvent innocence go free.

Patron of else the most despis'd of men,
Accept the tribute of a stranger's pen;
Verse, like the laurel, its immortal meed,
Should be the guerdon of a noble deed;
I may alarm thee, but I fear the shame
(Charity chosen as my theme and aim)

I must incur, forgetting HOWARD's name.*
Blest with all wealth can give thee, to resign
Joys doubly sweet to feelings quick as thine,
To quit the bliss thy rural scenes bestow,
To seek a nobler amidst scenes of woe,
To traverse seas, range kingdoms, and bring home,
Not the proud monuments of Greece or Rome,
But knowledge such as only dungeons teach,
And only sympathy like thine could reach;
That grief, sequester'd from the public stage,
Might smooth her feathers, and enjoy her cage;
Speaks a divine ambition, and a zeal,
The boldest patriot might be proud to feel.
Oh that the voice of clamour and debate,
That pleads for peace till it disturbs the state,
Were hushed in favour of thy gen'rous plea—
The poor thy clients, and Heaven's smile thy fee!

Philosophy, that does not dream or stray,
Walks arm in arm with nature all his way;
Compasses earth, dives into it, ascends
Whatever steep inquiry recommends,
Sees planetary wonders smoothly roll
Round other systems under her control,
Drinks wisdom at the milky stream of light,
That cheers the silent journey of the night,
And brings at his return a bosom charged
With rich instruction, and a soul enlarged.
The treasured sweets of the capacious plan,
That Heaven spreads wide before the view of man.
All prompt his pleased pursuit, and to pursue
Still prompt him, with a pleasure always new;
He, too, has a connecting pow'r, and draws
Man to the centre of the common cause;
Aiding a dubious and deficient sight

---

* John Howard (1726-90), the famous prison reformer, was an evangelical and
Calvinist whose *Statue of the Prisons* (1777) led to the reform act of the same year. The
Howard League for Penal Reform, forerunner of the contemporary John Howard Society,
was founded in his memory in 1866.

With a new medium and a purer light.
All truth is precious, if not all divine;
And what dilates the powers must needs refine.
He reads the skies, and, watching every change,
Provides the faculties an ampler range;
And wins mankind, as his attempts prevail,
A prouder station on the gen'ral scale.
But reason still, unless divinely taught,
Whate'er she learns, learns nothing as she ought;
The lamp of revelation only shows—
What human wisdom cannot but oppose—
That man, in nature's richest mantle clad,
And graced with all philosophy can add,
Though fair without, and luminous within,
Is still the progeny and heir of sin.
Thus taught, down falls the plumage of his pride;
He feels his need of an unerring guide,
And knows that, falling, he shall rise no more,
Unless the power that bade him stand restore.
This is indeed philosophy; this, known,
Makes wisdom, worthy of the name, his own;
And without this—whatever he discuss
Whether the space between the stars and us;
Whether he measure earth, compute the sea,
Weigh sunbeams, carve a fly, or spit a flea—
The solemn trifler, with his boasted skill
Toils much, and is a solemn trifler still:
Blind was he born, and his misguided eyes
Grown dim in trifling studies, blind he dies.
Self-knowledge, truly learn'd, of course implies
The rich possession of a nobler prize;
For self to self, and God to man, reveal'd
(Two themes to nature's eye for ever seal'd),
Are taught by rays, that fly with equal pace
From the same centre of enlight'ning grace.
Here stay thy foot—how copious and how clear,
Th' o'erflowing well of Charity springs here!
Hark! 'tis the music of a thousand rills,
Some through the groves, some down the sloping hills,

Winding a secret or an open course,
And all supplied from an eternal source.
The ties of nature do but feebly bind,
And commerce partially reclaims mankind;
Philosophy, without his heavenly guide,
May blow up self-conceit, and nourish pride;
But, while his province is the reas'ning part,
Has still a veil of midnight on his heart;*
'Tis truth divine, exhibited on earth,
Gives Charity her being and her birth.

Suppose (when thought is warm, and fancy flows,
What will not argument sometimes suppose?)
An isle possess'd by creatures of our kind,
Endued with reason, yet by nature blind.
Let supposition lend her aid once more,
And land some grave optician on the shore:
He claps his lens, if haply they may see,
Close to the part where vision ought to be;
But finds that, though his tubes assist the sight,
They cannot give it, or make darkness light.
He reads wise lectures, and describes aloud
A sense they know not to the wond'ring crowd;
He talks of light and the prismatic hues,
As men of depth in erudition use;
But all he gains for his harangue is—Well,
What monstrous lies some travellers will tell!

The soul, whose sight all-quick'ning grace renews,
Takes the resemblance of the good she views,
As diamonds, stripp'd of their opaque disguise,
Reflect the noon-day glory of the skies.
She speaks of Him, her author, guardian, friend,
Whose love knew no beginning, knows no end,
In language warm as all that love inspires;
And, in the glow of her intense desires,
Pants to communicate her noble fires.

---

*     Cf. 2 Corinthians 3:15.

She sees a world stark blind to what employs
Her eager thought,and feeds her flowing joys;
Though wisdom hail them, heedless of her call,
Flies to save some, and feels a pang for all:
Herself as weak as her support is strong,

She feels that frailty she denied so long;
And, from a knowledge of her own disease,
Learns to compassionate the sick she sees.
Here see, acquitted of all vain pretence,
The reign of genuine Charity commence.
Though scorn repay her sympathetic tears,
She still is kind, and still she perseveres;
The truth she loves a sightless world blaspheme—
'Tis childish dotage, a delirious dream!
The danger they discern not they deny;
Laugh at their only remedy, and die.
But still a soul thus touched can never cease,
Whoever threatens war, to speak of peace:
Pure in her aim, and in her temper mild,
Her wisdom seems the weakness of a child.
She makes excuses where she might condemn;
Reviled by those that hate her, prays for them;
Suspicion lurks not in her artless breast;
The worst suggested, she believes the best;
Not soon provoked, however stung and teased,
And, if perhaps made angry, soon appeased;
She rather waives than will dispute her right;
And, injured, makes forgiveness her delight.

Such was the portrait an apostle drew;
The bright original was one he knew;
Heaven held his hand—the likeness must be true.*

When one, that holds communion with the skies,
Has fill'd his urn where these pure waters rise,

---

*     The previous long passage describes the way in which a soul transformed by
redeeming grace takes on, by imitation, the attributes of love (Charity) described by the
Apostle Paul in 1 Corinthians, chapter 13.

And once more mingles with us meaner things,
'Tis e'en as if an angel shook his wings;
Immortal fragrance fills the circuit wide,
That tells us whence his treasures are supplied.
So, when a ship, well freighted with the stores
The sun matures on India's spicy shores,
Has dropt her anchor, and her canvas furled,
In some safe haven of our western world,
'Twere vain inquiry to what port she went;
The gale informs us, laden with the scent.

   Some seek, when queasy conscience has its qualms,
To lull the painful malady with alms;
But charity, not feigned, intends alone
Another's good*—theirs centres in their own;
And, too short-lived to reach the realms of peace,
Must cease for ever when the poor shall cease.
Flavia, most tender of her own good name,
Is rather careless of her sister's fame:
Her superfluity the poor supplies,
But, if she touch a character, it dies.
The seeming virtue weighed against the vice,
She deems all safe, for she has paid the price:
No charity but alms aught values she,
Except in porcelain on her mantel-tree.
How many deeds, with which the world has rung,
From pride, in league with ignorance, have sprung!
But God o'errules all human follies still,
And bends the tough materials to his will.
A conflagration—or a wintry flood,
Has left some hundreds without home or food:
Extravagance and avarice shall subscribe,
While fame and self-complacence are the bribe.
The brief proclaim'd, it visits every pew,
But first the squire's, a compliment but due:
With slow deliberation he unties
His glitt'ring purse—that envy of all eyes!

---

*     Cf. 1 Peter 1:22.

And, while the clerk just puzzles out the psalm,
Slides guinea behind guinea in his palm;
Till, finding (what he might have found before)
A smaller piece amidst the precious store,
Pinch'd close between his finger and his thumb,
He half exhibits, and then drops the sum.
Gold, to be sure!—Throughout the town 'tis told
How the good squire gives never less than gold.
From motives such as his, though not the best,
Springs in due time supply for the distress'd;
Not less effectual than what love bestows—
Except that office clips it as it goes.

But, lest I seem to sin against a friend,
And wound the grace I mean to recommend
(Though vice derided with a just design
Implies no trespass against love divine),
Once more I would adopt the graver style—
A teacher should be sparing of his smile.

Unless a love of virtue light the flame,
Satire is, more than those he brands, to blame:
He hides behind a magisterial air
His own offences, and strips others bare;
Affects indeed a most humane concern,
That men, if gently tutored, will not learn;
That mulish folly, not to be reclaimed
By softer methods, must be made ashamed;
But (I might instance in St. Patrick's dean)*
Too often rails to gratify his spleen.
Most satirists are indeed a public scourge;
Their mildest physic is a farrier's purge;
Their acrid temper turns, as soon as stirred,
The milk of their good purpose all to curd.
Their zeal begotten, as their works rehearse,
By lean despair upon an empty purse,
The wild assassins start into the street,

---

*    Jonathan Swift (1667-1745), Dean of St. Patrick's, Dublin, author of *Gulliver's Travels* (1726) and *Tale of a Tub* (1704).

Prepared to poniard whomsoe'er they meet,
No skill in swordmanship, however just,
Can be secure against a madman's thrust;
And even virtue, so unfairly matched,
Although immortal, may be pricked or scratched.
When scandal has new minted an old lie,
Or taxed invention for a fresh supply,
'Tis called a satire, and the world appears
Gathering around it with erected ears:
A thousand names are tossed into the crowd;
Some whispered softly, and some twanged aloud;
Just as the sapience of an author's brain
Suggests it safe or dang'rous to be plain.
Strange! how the frequent interjected dash
Quickens a market, and helps off the trash;
Th' important letters that include the rest,
Serve as key to those that are suppressed;
Conjecture gripes the victims in his paw,
The world is charmed, and Scrib* escapes the law.
So, when the cold damp shades of night prevail,
Worms may be caught by either head or tail;
Forcibly drawn from many a close recess,
They meet with little pity, no redress;
Plunged in the stream, they lodge upon the mud,
Food for the famished rovers of the flood.

All zeal for a reform, that gives offence
To peace and charity, is mere pretence:
A bold remark; but which, if well applied,
Would humble many a tow'ring poet's pride.
Perhaps the man was in a sportive fit,
And had no other play-place for his wit;
Perhaps, enchanted with the love of fame,
He sought the jewel in his neighbour's shame;
Perhaps—whatever end he might pursue,
The cause of virtue could not be his view.
At every stroke wit flashes in our eyes;

---

* A pseudonym for hack-journalists in general, some of whom were members of the "Scribblers' Club."

The turns are quick, the polish'd points surprise,
But shine with cruel and tremendous charms,
That, while they please, possess us with alarms;
So have I seen (and hasten'd to the sight
On all the wings of holiday delight)
Where stands that monument of ancient pow'r,
Named with emphatic dignity—the Tow'r,
Guns, halberts, swords, and pistols, great and small,
In starry forms dispos'd upon the wall.
We wonder, as we gazing stand below,
That brass and steel should make so fine a show;
But, though we praise th' exact designer's skill,
Account them implements of mischief still.

No works shall find acceptance, in that day
When all disguises shall be rent away,
That square not truly with the Scripture plan,
Nor spring from love to God, or love to man.
As he ordains things, sordid in their birth
To be resolv'd into their parent earth;
And, though the soul shall seek superior orbs,
Whate'er this world produces, it absorbs;
So self starts nothing, but what tends apace
Home to the goal where it began the race.
Such as our motive is our aim must be;
If this be servile, that can ne'er be free:
If self employ us, whatsoe'er is wrought,
We glorify that self, not Him we ought;
Such virtues had need prove their own reward,
The Judge of all men owes them no regard.
True Charity, a plant divinely nursed,
Fed by the love from which it rose at first,
Thrives against hope, and, in the rudest scene,
Storms but enliven its unfading green;
Exub'rant is the shadow it supplies;
Its fruit on earth, its growth above the skies.
To look at Him, who formed us and redeemed,
So glorious now, though once so disesteemed;
To see a God stretch forth his human hand,

To uphold the boundless scenes of his command:
To recollect that, in a form like ours,
He bruis'd beneath his feet th' infernal powers,[*]
Captivity led captive,[†] rose to claim
The wreath he won so dearly in our name;
That, throned above all height, he condescends
To call the few that trust in him his friends;
That, in the heaven of heavens, that space he deems
Too scanty for th' exertion of his beams,
And shines, as if impatient to bestow
Life and a kingdom upon worms below;
That sight imparts a never-dying flame,
Though feeble in degree, in kind the same.
Like him, the soul, thus kindled from above,
Spreads wide her arms of universal love;
And, still enlarged as she receives the grace,
Includes creation in her close embrace.
Behold a Christian!—and, without the fires
The Founder of that name alone inspires,
Though all accomplishment, all knowledge meet,
To make the shining prodigy complete,
Whoever boast that name—behold a cheat!

Were love, in these the world's last doting years,
As frequent as the want of it appears,
The churches warm'd, they would no longer hold
Such frozen figures, stiff as they are cold;
Relenting forms would lose their power, or cease;
And e'en the dipped and sprinkled live in peace:[†]
Each heart would quit its prison in the breast,
And flow in free communion with the rest.
And statesman, skilled in projects dark and deep,
Might burn his useless Machiavel, and sleep;
His budget, often filled, yet always poor,
Might swing at ease behind his study door,
No longer prey upon our annual rents,

---

[*]    Cf. Romans 16:20.
[†]    Psalm 68:18; Ephesians 4:8.
[‡]    Baptists, and all other Christians.

Or scare the nation with its big contents:
Disbanded legions freely might depart,
And slaying man would cease to be an art.
No learned disputants would take the field,
Sure not to conquer, and sure not to yield;
Both sides deceived, if rightly understood,
Pelting each other for the public good.
Did Charity prevail, the press would prove
A vehicle of virtue, truth, and love;
And I might spare myself the pains to shew
What few can learn, and all suppose they know.

Thus have I sought to grace a serious lay
With many a wild, indeed, but flow'ry spray,
In hopes to gain, what else I must have lost,
The attention pleasure has so much engross'd.
But if, unhappily deceived, I dream,
And prove too weak for so divine a theme,
Let Charity forgive me a mistake,
That zeal, not vanity, has chanced to make,
And spare the poet for his subject's sake.

# THE TASK (1781)

## ADVERTISEMENT

THE history of the following production is briefly this— A
lady (Lady Austen), fond of blank verse, demanded a
poem of that kind from the author, and gave him the
Sofa for a subject. He obeyed; and, having much leisure,
connected another subject with it; and, pursuing the train
of thought to which his situation and turn of mind led
him, brought forth at length, instead of the trifle which he
at first intended, a serious affair—a Volume!

In the poem on the subject of Education he would be very
sorry to stand suspected of having aimed his censure

84

*at any particular school. His objections are such as naturally apply themselves to schools in general. If there were not, as for the most part there is, wilful neglect in those who manage them, and an omission even of such discipline as they are susceptible of, the objects are yet too numerous for minute attention; and the aching hearts of ten thousand parents, mourning under the bitterest of all disappointments, attest the truth of the allegation. His quarrel, therefore, is with the mischief at large, and not with any particular instance of it.*

# BOOK III—THE GARDEN

## THE ARGUMENT

*SELF-recollection and reproof—Address to domestic happiness—Some account of myself—The vanity of many of their pursuits who are reputed wise—Justification of my censures—Divine illumination necessary to the most expert philosopher—The question, What is truth? answered by other questions—Domestic happiness addressed again— Few lovers of the country—My tame hare—Occupations of a retired gentleman in his garden—Pruning—Framing— Greenhouse—Sowing of flower seeds—The country preferable to the town even in the winter—Reasons why it is deserted at that season—Ruinous effects of gaming and of expensive improvement—Book concludes with an apostrophe to the metropolis.*

As one who, long in thickets and in brakes
Entangled, winds now this way and now that
His devious course uncertain, seeking home;
Or, having long in miry ways been foiled,
And sore discomfited, from slough to slough
Plunging, and half despairing of escape;
If chance at length he finds a greensward smooth

And faithful to the foot, his spirits rise,
He chirrups brisk his ear-erecting steed,
And winds his way with pleasure and with ease:
So I, designing other themes, and called
To adorn the Sofa with eulogium due,
To tell its slumbers, and to paint its dreams,
Have rambled wide. In country, city, seat
Of academic fame (howe'er deserved),
Long held, and scarcely disengaged at last.
But now, with pleasant pace, a cleanlier road
I mean to tread. I feel myself at large,
Courageous, and refreshed for future toil,
If toil awaits me, or if dangers new.

   Since pulpits fail, and sounding boards reflect
Most part an empty ineffectual sound,
What chance that I, to fame so little known,
Nor conversant with men or manners much,
Should speak to purpose, or with better hope
Crack the satiric thong? 'Twere wiser far
For me, enamoured of sequestered scenes,
And charmed with rural beauty, to repose,
Where chance may throw me, beneath elm or vine,
My languid limbs, when summer sears the plains;
Or, when rough winter rages, on the soft
And sheltered Sofa, while the nitrous air
Feeds a blue flame, and makes a cheerful hearth;
There, undisturbed by folly, and apprised
How great the danger of disturbing her,
To muse in silence, or at least confine
Remarks that gall so many to the few,
My partners in retreat. Disgust concealed
Is oft-times proof of wisdom, when the fault
Is obstinate, and cure beyond our reach.

   Domestic happiness, thou only bliss
Of Paradise that has survived the fall!
Though few now taste thee unimpaired and pure,
Or tasting long enjoy thee; too infirm,

Or too incautious, to preserve thy sweets
Unmix'd with drops of bitter, which neglect
Or, temper, sheds into thy crystal cup;
Thou art the nurse of Virtue—in thine arms
She smiles, appearing, as in truth she is,
Heaven-born, and destined to the skies again.
Thou art not known where Pleasure is adored,
That reeling goddess with the zoneless waist
And wand'ring eyes, still leaning on the arm
Of novelty, her fickle frail support;
For thou art meek and constant, hating change,
And finding, in the calm of truth-tried love
Joys that her stormy raptures never yield.
Forsaking thee, what shipwreck have we made
Of honour, dignity, and fair renown!
Till prostitution elbows us aside
In all our crowded streets; and senates seem
Convened for purposes of empire less
Than to release th' adultress from her bond.
The adultress! what a theme for angry verse!
What provocation to th' indignant heart,
That feels for injur'd love! but I disdain
The nauseous task, to paint her as she is,
Cruel, abandon'd, glorying in her shame!
No:—let her pass, and, charioted along
In guilty splendour, shake the public ways;
The frequency of crimes has wash'd them white!
And verse of mine shall never brand the wretch,
Whom matrons now, of character unsmirch'd,
And chaste themselves, are not ashamed to own.
Virtue and vice had bound'ries in old time,
Not to be passed: and she, that had renounced
Her sex's honour, was renounced herself
By all that prized it; not for prud'ry's sake,
But dignity's, resentful of the wrong.
'Twas hard, perhaps, on here and there a waif,
Desirous to return, and not received;
But was a wholesome rigour in the main,
And taught th' unblemished to preserve with care

That purity, whose loss was loss of all.
Men, too, were nice in honour in those days,
And judg'd offenders well. Then he that sharp'd,
And pocketed a prize by fraud obtain'd,
Was marked and shunned as odious. He that sold
His country, or was slack when she required
His ev'ry nerve in action and at stretch,
Paid, with the blood that he had basely spared,
The price of his default. But now—yes, now
We are become so candid and so fair,
So lib'ral in construction, and so rich
In Christian charity (good-natured age!),
That they are safe, sinners of either sex,
Transgress what laws they may. Well dressed, well bred,
Well equipaged, is ticket good enough
To pass us readily through ev'ry door.
Hypocrisy, detest her as we may
(And no man's hatred ever wronged her yet),
May claim this merit still—that she admits
The worth of what she mimics with such care,
And thus gives virtue indirect applause;
But she has burnt her mask, not needed here,
Where vice has such allowance, that her shifts
And specious semblances have lost their use.

I was a stricken deer, that left the herd
Long since; with many an arrow deep infixt
My panting side was charged, when I withdrew,
To seek a tranquil death in distant shades.*
There was I found by One who had himself
Been hurt by the archers. In his side he bore,
And in his hands and feet, the cruel scars.
With gentle force soliciting the darts,
He drew them forth, and healed, and bade me live.
Since then, with few associates, in remote
And silent woods I wander, far from those

---

*     Though there are biblical overtones (e.g., Psalm 42:1), the allusion is to a figure familiar from Virgil (*Aeneid* 4.68-73), Spenser (*Faerie Queene* 2.1.12) and others. Original to Cowper is his analogy with Christ as Man of Sorrows.

My former partners of the peopled scene;
With few associates, not wishing more.
Here much I ruminate, as much I may,
With other views of men and manners now
Than once, and others of a life to come.
I see that all are wand'rers, gone astray
Each in his own delusions; they are lost
In chase of fancied happiness, still woo'd
And never won. Dream after dream ensues;
And still they dream that they shall still succeed;
And still are disappointed.  Rings the world
With the vain stir.  I sum up half mankind,
And add two-thirds of the remaining half,
And find the total of their hopes and fears
Dreams, empty dreams.  The million flit as gay
As if created only like the fly,
That spreads his motley wings in the eye of noon,
To sport their season, and be seen no more.
The rest are sober dreamers, grave and wise,
And pregnant with discov'ries new and rare.
Some write a narrative of wars, and feats
Of heroes little known; and call the rant
An history: describe the man, of whom
His own coevals took but little note;
And paint his person, character, and views,
As they had known him from his mother's womb.
They disentangle from the puzzled skein,
In which obscurity has wrapped them up,
The threads of politic and shrewd design,
That ran through all his purposes, and charge
His mind with meanings that he never had,
Or, having, kept concealed.  Some drill and bore
The solid earth, and from the strata there
Extract a register, by which we learn,
That He who made it, and reveal'd its date
To Moses, was mistaken in its age.
Some, more acute, and more industrious still,
Contrive creation; travel nature up
To the sharp peak of her sublimest height,

And tell us whence the stars; why some are fix'd,
And planetary some; what gave them first
Rotation, from what fountain flowed their light.
Great contest follows, and much learned dust
Involves the combatants; each claiming truth,
And truth disclaiming both.  And thus they spend
The little wick of life's poor shallow lamp
In playing tricks with nature, giving laws
To distant worlds, and trifling in their own.
Is't not a pity, now, that tickling rheums
Should ever tease the lungs and blear the sight
Of oracles like these?  Great pity too,
That, having wielded the elements, and built
A thousand systems, each in his own way,
They should go out in fume, and be forgot?
Ah! what is life thus spent? and what are they
But frantic who thus spend it? all for smoke—
Eternity for bubbles proves at last
A senseless bargain.  When I see such games
Play'd by the creatures of a Power who swears
That he will judge the earth, and call the fool
To a sharp reck'ning that has lived in vain;
And when I weigh this seeming wisdom well,
And prove it in th' infallible result
So hollow and so false—I feel my heart
Dissolve in pity, and account the learned,
If this be learning, most of all deceived.
Great crimes alarm the conscience, but it sleeps
While thoughtful man is plausibly amus'd.
Defend me, therefore, common sense, say I,
From reveries so airy, from the toil
Of dropping buckets into empty wells,
And growing old in drawing nothing up!

　'Twere well, says one sage erudite, profound,
Terribly arch'd and aquiline his nose,
And overbuilt with most impending brows,
'Twere well, could you permit the world to live
As the world pleases: what's the world to you?—

Much. I was born of woman, and drew milk,
As sweet as charity from human breasts.
I think, articulate, I laugh and weep,
And exercise all functions of a man.
How then should I and any man that lives
Be strangers to each other? Pierce my vein,
Take of the crimson stream meand'ring there,
And catechise it well; apply thy glass,
Search it, and prove now if it be not blood
Congenial with thine own: and, if it be,
What edge of subtlety canst thou suppose
Keen enough, wise and skilful as thou art,
To cut the link of brotherhood, by which
One common Maker bound me to the kind?
True; I am no proficient, I confess,
In arts like yours. I cannot call the swift
And perilous lightnings from the angry clouds,
And bid them hide themselves in earth beneath;
I cannot analyse the air, nor catch
The parallax of yonder luminous point,
That seems half-quenched in the immense abyss:
Such pow'rs I boast not—neither can I rest
A silent witness of the headlong rage
Or heedless folly by which thousands die,
Bone of my bone, and kindred souls to mine.

  God never meant that man should scale the heavens
By strides of human wisdom. In his works
Though wondrous, he commands us in his word
To seek *him*, rather, where his mercy shines.
The mind indeed, enlightened from above,
Views him in all; ascribes to the grand cause
The grand effect; acknowledges with joy
His manner, and with rapture tastes his style.
But never yet did philosophic tube,
That brings the planets home into the eye
Of observation, and discovers, else
Not visible, his family of worlds,
Discover him that rules them; such a veil

Hangs over mortal eyes, blind from the birth,
And dark in things divine.  Full often, too,
Our wayward intellect, the more we learn
Of nature, overlooks her Author more;
From instrumental causes proud to draw
Conclusions retrograde, and mad mistake.
But if his word once teach us, shoot a ray
Through all the heart's dark chambers, and reveal
Truths undiscerned but by that holy light,
Then all is plain.  Philosophy, baptized
In the pure fountain of eternal love,
Has eyes indeed; and, viewing all she sees
As meant to indicate a God to man,
Gives *him* his praise, and forfeits not her own.
Learning has borne such fruit in other days
On all her branches: piety has found
Friends in the friends of science, and true pray'r
Has flowed from lips wet with Castalian dews.
Such was thy wisdom, Newton, child-like sage!
Sagacious reader of the works of God,
And in his word sagacious.*  Such too thine,
Milton, whose genius had angelic wings,
And fed on manna!  And such thine, in whom
Our British Themis gloried with just cause,
Immortal Hale!† for deep discernment praised,
And sound integrity, not more than famed
For sanctity of manners undefiled.

All flesh is grass, and all its glory fades
Like the fair flow'r dishevelled in the wind;
Riches have wings, and grandeur is a dream:
The man we celebrate must find a tomb,
And we that worship him ignoble graves.
Nothing is proof against the gen'ral curse
Of vanity, that seizes all below.
The only amaranthine flow'r on earth

---

\*    A reference to Isaac Newton's *Observations on the Prophecies of Daniel and the Apocalypse of St. John* (1733).
†    Sir Matthew Hale (1609-76), respected judge, author, and friend of Richard Baxter.

Is virtue; th' only lasting treasure, truth.
But what is truth? 'Twas Pilate's question put
To Truth itself, that deigned him no reply.
And wherefore? will not God impart his light
To them that ask it?—Freely—'tis his joy,
His glory, and his nature to impart.
But to the proud, uncandid, insincere,
Or negligent inquirer not a spark.
What's that which brings contempt upon a book,
And him who writes it, though the style be neat,
The method clear, and argument exact?
That makes a minister in holy things
The joy of many and the dread of more,
His name a theme for praise and for reproach?—
That, while it gives us worth in God's account,
Depreciates and undoes us in our own?
What pearl is it that rich men cannot buy,
That learning is too proud to gather up;
But which the poor, and the despised of all,
Seek and obtain, and often find unsought?
Tell me—and I will tell thee what is truth.

O, friendly to the best pursuits of man,
Friendly to thought, to virtue, and to peace,
Domestic life in rural leisure passed!
Few know thy value, and few taste thy sweets;
Though many boast thy favours, and affect
To understand and choose thee for their own.
But foolish man forgoes his proper bliss,
E'en as his first progenitor, and quits,
Though placed in Paradise (for earth has still
Some traces of her youthful beauty left),
Substantial happiness for transient joy.
Scenes formed for contemplation, and to nurse
The growing seeds of wisdom; that suggest,
By ev'ry pleasing image they present,
Reflections such as meliorate the heart,
Compose the passions, and exalt the mind;
Scenes such as these 'tis his supreme delight

To fill with riot, and defile with blood.
Should some contagion, kind to the poor brutes
We persecute, annihilate the tribes
That draw the sportsman over hill and dale,
Fearless, and rapt away from all his cares;
Should never game-fowl hatch her eggs again,
Nor baited hook deceive the fish's eye;
Could pageantry and dance, and feast and song,
Be quell'd in all our summer-months' retreat,
How many self-deluded nymphs and swains,
Who dream they have a taste for fields and groves,
Would find them hideous nurs'ries of the spleen,
And crowd the roads, impatient for the town!
They love the country, and none else, who seek
For their own sake its silence and its shade.
Delights which who would leave, that has a heart
Susceptible of pity, or a mind
Cultured and capable of sober thought,
For all the savage din of the swift pack,
And clamours of the field?—Detested sport,
That owes its pleasures to another's pain;
That feeds upon the sobs and dying shrieks
Of harmless nature, dumb, but yet endued
With eloquence, that agonies inspire
Of silent tears and heart-distending sighs?
Vain tears, alas! and sighs, that never find
A corresponding tone in jovial souls!
Well—one at least is safe. One shelter'd hare
Has never heard the sanguinary yell
Of cruel man, exulting in her woes.
Innocent partner of my peaceful home,
Whom ten long years' experience of my care
Has made at last familiar; she has lost
Much of her vigilant instinctive dread,
Not needful here, beneath a roof like mine.
Yes—thou may'st eat thy bread, and lick the hand
That feeds thee; thou mayest frolic on the floor
At evening, and at night retire secure
To thy straw couch, and slumber unalarm'd;

For I have gain'd thy confidence, have pledged
All that is human in me to protect
Thine unsuspecting gratitude and love.
If I survive thee, I will dig thy grave;
And, when I place thee in it, sighing, say,
I knew at least one hare that had a friend.*

How various his employments whom the world
Calls idle; and who justly, in return
Esteems that busy world an idler too!
Friends, books, a garden, and perhaps his pen,
Delightful industry enjoyed at home,
And Nature, in her cultivated trim
Dressed to his taste, inviting him abroad—
Can he want occupation who has these?
Will he be idle who has much t' enjoy?
Me, therefore, studious of laborious ease,
Not slothful; happy to deceive the time,
Not waste it; and aware that human life
Is but a loan to be repaid with use,
When He shall call his debtors to account†
From whom are all our blessings, bus'ness finds
E'en here: while sedulous I seek t' improve,
At least neglect not, or leave unemploy'd,
The mind He gave me; driving it, though slack
Too oft, and much impeded in its work
By causes not to be divulged in vain,
To its just point—the service of mankind.
He, that attends to his interior self,
That has a heart, and keeps it; has a mind
That hungers, and supplies it; and who seeks
A social, not a dissipated life,
Has business; feels himself engaged t' achieve
No unimportant, though a silent, task.
A life all turbulence and noise may seem
To him that leads it, wise, and to be praised;
But wisdom is a pearl with most success

---

*    Cf. John Gay's fable, "The Hare and many Friends."
†    Cf. Matthew 25:14-30.

Sought in still water, and beneath clear skies.
He that is ever occupied in storms,
Or dives not for it, or brings up instead,
Vainly industrious, a disgraceful prize.

   The morning finds the self-sequestered man
Fresh for his task, intend what task he may.
Whether inclement seasons recommend
His warm but simple home, where he enjoys
With her who shares his pleasures and his heart,
Sweet converse, sipping calm the fragrant lymph
Which neatly she prepares; then to his book,
Well chosen, and not sullenly perused
In selfish silence, but imparted oft
As ought occurs that she might smile to hear,
Or turn to nourishment, digested well.
Or, if the garden with its many cares,
All well repaid, demand him, he attends
The welcome call, conscious how much the hand
Of lubbard Labour needs his watchful eye.
Oft loitering lazily, if not o'erseen,
Or misapplying his unskilful strength.
Nor does he govern only or direct,
But much performs himself. No works, indeed,
That ask robust, tough sinews, bred to toil,
Servile employ; but such as may amuse,
Not tire, demanding rather skill than force.
Proud of his well-spread walls, he views his trees
That meet (no barren interval between)
With pleasure more than e'en their fruits afford,
Which, save himself who trains them, none can feel:
These, therefore, are his own peculiar charge;
No meaner hand may discipline the shoots,
None but his steel approach them. What is weak,
Distemper'd, or has lost prolific pow'rs,
Impair'd by age, his unrelenting hand
Dooms to the knife: nor does he spare the soft
And succulent, that feeds its giant growth,
But barren, at th' expense of neighb'ring twigs

Less ostentatious, and yet studded thick
With hopeful gems.  The rest, no portion left
That may disgrace his art, or disappoint
Large expectations, he disposes neat,
At measured distances, that air and sun,
Admitted freely, may afford their aid,
And ventilate and warm the swelling buds.
Hence summer has her riches, autumn hence,
And hence e'en winter fills his wither'd hand
With blushing fruits, and plenty, not his own.
Fair recompence of labour well bestowed,
And wise precaution; which a clime so rude
Makes needful still, whose spring is but the child
Of churlish winter, in her froward moods
Discov'ring much the temper of her sire.
For oft, as if in her the stream of mild
Maternal nature had reversed its course,
She brings her infants forth with many smiles;
But, once deliver'd, kills them with a frown.
He, therefore, timely warned himself, supplies
Her want of care, screening and keeping warm
The plenteous bloom, that no rough blast may sweep
His garlands from the boughs.  Again, as oft
As the sun peeps and vernal airs breathe mild,
The fence withdrawn, he gives them ev'ry beam,
And spreads his hopes before the blaze of day.

   To raise the prickly and green-coated gourd,
So grateful to the palate, and when rare
So coveted, else base and disesteemed—
Food for the vulgar merely—is an art
That toiling ages have but just matured,
And at this moment unassayed in song.
Yet gnats have had, and frogs and mice, long since,
Their eulogy; those sang the Mantuan bard;*
And these the Grecian,† in ennobling strains;

---

*     Virgil
†     Homer

And in thy numbers, Phillips,* shines for aye,
The solitary shilling.  Pardon then,
Ye sage dispensers of poetic fame,
Th' ambition of one, meaner far, whose pow'rs,
Presuming an attempt not less sublime,
Pant for the praise of dressing to the taste
Of critic appetite, no sordid fare,
A cucumber, while costly yet and scarce.

    The stable yields a stercoraceous heap,
Impregnated with quick fermenting salts,
And potent to resist the freezing blast:
For, ere the beech and elm have cast their leaf
Deciduous, when now November dark
Checks vegetation in the torpid plant
Exposed to his cold breath, the task begins.
Warily, therefore, and with prudent heed,
He seeks a favour'd spot; that where he builds
The agglomerated pile his frame may front
The sun's meridian disk, and at the back
Enjoy close shelter, wall, or reeds, or hedge
Impervious to the wind.  First he bids spread
Dry fern or litter'd hay, that may imbibe
The ascending damps; then leisurely impose,
And lightly, shaking it with agile hand
From the full fork, the saturated straw.
What longest binds the closest forms secure
The shapely side, that as it rises takes,
By just degrees, an overhanging breadth,
Shelt'ring the base with its projected eaves:
Th' uplifted frame, compact at ev'ry joint,
And overlaid with clear translucent glass,
He settles next upon the sloping mount,
Whose sharp declivity shoots off secure
From the dashed pane the deluge as it falls.
He shuts it close, and the first labour ends.
Thrice must the voluble and restless earth

---

\*      John Philips (1676-1708), wrote a mock-heroic poem, *The Splendid Shilling* (1703).

Spin round upon her axle, ere the warmth,
Slow gathering in the midst, through the square mass
Diffused, attain the surface: when, behold!
A pestilent and most corrosive steam,
Like a gross fog Bœotian, rising fast,
And fast condensed upon the dewy sash,
Asks egress; which obtained, the overcharged
And drenched conservatory breathes abroad,
In volumes wheeling slow, the vapour dank;
And, purified, rejoices to have lost
Its foul inhabitant.  But to assuage
Th' impatient fervour, which it first conceives
Within its reeking bosom, threatening death
To his young hopes, requires discreet delay.
Experience, slow preceptress, teaching oft
The way to glory by miscarriage foul,
Must prompt him, and admonish how to catch
Th' auspicious moment, when the temper'd heat,
Friendly to vital motion, may afford
Soft fomentation, and invite the seed.
The seed, selected wisely, plump, and smooth,
And glossy, he commits to pots of size
Diminutive, well filled with well prepared
And fruitful soil, that has been treasured long,
And drunk no moisture from the dripping clouds:
These on the warm and genial earth, that hides
The smoking manure and o'erspreads it all,
He places lightly, and, as time subdues
The rage of fermentation, plunges deep
In the soft medium, till they stand immersed.
Then rise the tender germs, upstarting quick,
And spreading wide their spongy lobes; at first
Pale, wan, and livid; but assuming soon,
If fanned by balmy and nutritious air,
Strained through the friendly mats, a vivid green.
Two leaves produced, two rough indented leaves,
Cautious he pinches from the second stalk
A pimple, that portends a future sprout,
And interdicts its growth.  Thence straight succeed

The branches, sturdy to his utmost wish;
Prolific all, and harbingers of more.
The crowded roots demand enlargement now,
And transplantation in an ampler space.
Indulged in what they wish, they soon supply
Large foliage, overshadowing golden flow'rs,
Blown on the summit of th' apparent fruit.
These have their sexes; and, when summer shines,
The bee transports the fertilizing meal
From flow'r to flow'r, and e'en the breathing air
Wafts the rich prize to its appointed use.
Not so when winter scowls. Assistant Art
Then acts in Nature's office, brings to pass
The glad espousals, and ensures the crop.

   Grudge not, ye rich (since luxury must have
His dainties, and the World's more num'rous half
Lives by contriving delicates for you),
Grudge not the cost. Ye little know the cares,
The vigilance, the labour, and the skill,
That day and night are exercised, and hang
Upon the ticklish balance of suspense,
That ye may garnish your profuse regales
With summer fruits brought forth by wintry suns.
Ten thousand dangers lie in wait to thwart
The process. Heat, and cold, and wind, and steam,
Moisture and drought, mice, worms, and swarming flies,
Minute as dust, and numberless, oft work
Dire disappointment, that admits no cure,
And which no care can obviate. It were long,
Too long, to tell th' expedients and the shifts
Which he that fights a season so severe
Devises while he guards his tender trust;
And oft, at last in vain. The learn'd and wise
Sarcastic would exclaim, and judge the song
Cold as its theme, and, like its theme, the fruit
Of too much labour, worthless when produc'd.

Who loves a garden loves a greenhouse too.
Unconscious of a less propitious clime,
There blooms exotic beauty, warm and snug,
While the winds whistle and the snows descend.
The spiry myrtle with unwith'ring leaf
Shines there, and flourishes. The golden boast
Of Portugal and western India there,
The ruddier orange, and the paler lime,
Peep through their polish'd foliage at the storm,
And seem to smile at what they need not fear.
Th' amomum there with intermingling flowers
And cherries hangs her twigs. Geranium boasts
Her crimson honours, and the spangled beau,
Ficoides, glitters bright the winter long.
All plants, of ev'ry leaf, that can endure
The winter's frown, if screen'd from his shrewd bite,
Live there, and prosper. Those Ausonia claims,
Levantine regions these; th' Azores send
Their jessamine, her jessamine remote
Caffraria: foreigners from many lands,
They form one social shade, as if convened
By magic summons of th' Orphean lyre.
Yet just arrangement, rarely brought to pass
But by a master's hand, disposing well
The gay diversities of leaf and flower,
Must lend its aid to illustrate all their charms,
And dress the regular yet various scene.
Plant behind plant aspiring, in the van
The dwarfish, in the rear retired, but still
Sublime above the rest, the statelier stand.
So once were ranged the sons of ancient Rome,
A noble show! while Roscius* trod the stage;
And so, while Garrick,† as renowned as he,
The sons of Albion; fearing each to lose
Some note of Nature's music from his lips,
And covetous of Shakspeare's beauty, seen
In ev'ry flash of his far-beaming eye.

---

*    Ex-slave who became a famous Roman actor, defended by Cicero.
†    English Shakespearean actor (1717-1779).

Nor taste alone and well-contrived display
Suffice to give the marshall'd ranks the grace
Of their complete effect.  Much yet remains
Unsung, and many cares are yet behind,
And more laborious; cares on which depends
Their vigour, injured soon, not soon restored.
The soil must be renewed, which, often washed,
Loses its treasure of salubrious salts,
And disappoints the roots; the slender roots
Close interwoven, where they meet the vase,
Must smooth be shorn away; the sapless branch
Must fly before the knife; the wither'd leaf
Must be detach'd, and where it strews the floor
Swept with a woman's neatness, breeding else
Contagion, and disseminating death.
Discharge but these kind offices (and who
Would spare, that loves them, offices like these?)
Well they reward the toil.  The sight is pleased,
The scent regaled, each odorif'rous leaf,
Each opening blossom freely breathes abroad
Its gratitude, and thanks him with its sweets.

   So manifold, all pleasing in their kind,
All healthful, are th' employs of rural life,
Reiterated as the wheel of time
Runs round; still ending and beginning still.
Nor are these all.  To deck the shapely knoll,
That softly swelled and gaily dressed appears
A flowery island, from the dark green lawn
Emerging, must be deem'd a labour due
To no mean hand, and asks the touch of taste.
Here also grateful mixture of well-match'd
And sorted hues (each giving each relief,
And by contrasted beauty shining more)
Is needful.  Strength may wield the pond'rous spade,
May turn the clod, and wheel the compost home;
But elegance, chief grace the garden shows,
And most attractive, is the fair result
Of thought, the creature of a polish'd mind.

Without it all is gothic as the scene
To which th' insipid citizen resorts
Near yonder heath; where industry misspent,
But proud of his uncouth ill-chosen task,
Has made a heaven on earth; with suns and moons
Of close rammed stones has charged the encumbered soil,
And fairly laid the zodiac in the dust.
He therefore, who would see his flowers disposed
Sightly and in just order, ere he gives
The beds the trusted treasure of their seeds,
Forecasts the future whole; that, when the scene
Shall break into its preconceived display,
Each for itself, and all as with one voice
Conspiring, may attest his bright design.
Nor even then, dismissing as perform'd
His pleasant work, may he suppose it done.
Few self-supported flowers endure the wind
Uninjured, but expect th' upholding aid
Of the smooth-shaven prop, and, neatly tied,
Are wedded thus, like beauty to old age,
For int'rest sake, the living to the dead.
Some clothe the soil that feeds them, far diffused
And lowly creeping, modest and yet fair,
Like virtue, thriving most where little seen;
Some, more aspiring, catch the neighbour shrub
With clasping tendrils, and invest his branch,
Else unadorn'd, with many a gay festoon
And fragrant chaplet, recompensing well
The strength they borrow with the grace they lend.
All hate the rank society of weeds,
Noisome, and ever greedy to exhaust
The impov'rished earth; an overbearing race,
That, like the multitude made faction-mad,
Disturb good order, and degrade true worth.

Oh, blest seclusion from a jarring world,
Which he, thus occupied, enjoys!  Retreat
Cannot indeed to guilty man restore
Lost innocence, or cancel follies past;

But it has peace, and much secures the mind
From all assaults of evil; proving still
A faithful barrier, not o'erleap'd with ease
By vicious Custom, raging uncontroll'd
Abroad, and desolating public life.
When fierce temptation, seconded within
By traitor appetite, and arm'd with darts
Temper'd in Hell, invades the throbbing breast,
To combat may be glorious, and success
Perhaps may crown us; but to fly is safe.
Had I the choice of sublunary good,
What could I wish, that I possess not here?
Health, leisure, means t' improve it, friendship, peace,
No loose or wanton, though a wand'ring, muse,
And constant occupation without care.
Thus blest, I draw a picture of that bliss;
Hopeless indeed, that dissipated minds,
And profligate abusers of a world
Created fair so much in vain for them,
Should seek the guiltless joys that I describe,
Allured by my report: but sure no less
That, self-condemn'd, they must neglect the prize,
And what they will not taste must yet approve.
What we admire we praise; and, when we praise,
Advance it into notice, that, its worth
Acknowledged, others may admire it too.
I therefore recommend, though at the risk
Of popular disgust, yet boldly still,
The cause of piety and sacred truth,
And virtue, and those scenes which God ordain'd
Should best secure them and promote them most,
Scenes that I love, and with regret perceive
Forsaken, or through folly not enjoyed.
Pure is the nymph, though lib'ral of her smiles,
And chaste, though unconfined, whom I extol.
Not as the prince in Shushan,* when he called,
Vain-glorious of her charms, his Vashti forth,

---

*     Esther 1:1-12.

To grace the full pavilion.  His design
Was but to boast his own peculiar good,
Which all might view with envy, none partake.
My charmer is not mine alone; my sweets,
And she that sweetens all my bitters too,
Nature, enchanting Nature, in whose form
And lineaments divine I trace a hand
That errs not, and finds raptures still renew'd,
Is free to all men—universal prize.
Strange that so fair a creature should yet want
Admirers, and be destined to divide
With meaner objects e'en the few she finds!
Stripped of her ornaments, her leaves, and flowers,
She loses all her influence.  Cities then
Attract us, and neglected Nature pines,
Abandoned, as unworthy of our love.
But are not wholesome airs, though unperfumed
By roses; and clear suns, though scarcely felt;
And groves, if unharmonious, yet secure
From clamour, and whose very silence charms;
To be preferr'd to smoke, to the eclipse
That metropolitan volcanoes make,
Whose Stygian* throats breathe darkness all day long;
And to the stir of commerce, driving slow,
And thund'ring loud, with his ten thousand wheels?
They would be, were not madness in the head,
And folly in the heart; were England now
What England was, plain hospitable, kind,
And undebauched.  But we have bid farewell
To all the virtues of those better days,
And all their honest pleasures.  Mansions once
Knew their own masters; and laborious hinds
Who had survived the father, served the son.
Now the legitimate and rightful lord
Is but a transient guest, newly arrived,
And soon to be supplanted.  He that saw
His patrimonial timber cast its leaf

---

*    Referring to the impenetrable underworld gloom of the river Styx.

Sells the last scantling, and transfers the price
To some shrewd sharper, ere it buds again.
Estates are landscapes, gazed upon awhile,
Then advertised, and auctioneered away.
The country starves, and they that feed the o'ercharged
And surfeited lewd town with her fair dues,
By a just judgment strip and starve themselves.
The wings that waft our riches out of sight
Grow on the gamester's elbows; and th' alert
And nimble motion of those restless joints,
That never tire, soon fans them all away.
Improvement too, the idol of the age,
Is fed with many a victim.  Lo, he comes!
Th' omnipotent magician, Brown,* appears!
Down falls the venerable pile, th' abode
Of our forefathers—a grave whiskered race,
But tasteless.  Springs a palace in its stead,
But in a distant spot; where, more exposed,
It may enjoy the advantage of the north,
And aguish east, till time shall have transform'd
Those naked acres to a shelt'ring grove.
He speaks.  The lake in front becomes a lawn;
Woods vanish, hills subside, and valleys rise:
And streams, as if created for his use,
Pursue the track of his directing wand,
Sinuous or straight, now rapid and now slow,
Now murm'ring soft, now roaring in cascades—
E'en as he bids!  Th' enraptured owner smiles.
'Tis finished, and yet, finished as it seems,
Still wants a grace, the loveliest it could show,
A mine to satisfy the enormous cost.
Drained to the last poor item of his wealth,
He sighs, departs, and leaves the accomplished plan,
That he has touched, retouched, many a long day
Labour'd, and many a night pursued in dreams,
Just when it meets his hopes, and proves the heaven
He wanted, for a wealthier to enjoy!

---

*    Lancelot "Capability" Brown (1716-1783) was the leading landscape gardener of the
eighteenth-century, and raised such work to a high art.

And now perhaps the glorious hour is come,
When, having no stake left, no pledge t' endear
Her int'rests, or that gives her sacred cause
A moment's operation on his love,
He burns with most intense and flagrant zeal,
To serve his country.  Ministerial grace
Deals him out money from the public chest;
Or, if that mine be shut, some private purse
Supplies his need with a usurious loan,
To be refunded duly when his vote,
Well-managed, shall have earned its worthy price.
Oh innocent, compared with arts like these,
Crape, and cock'd pistol, and the whistling ball
Sent through the traveller's temples! He that finds
One drop of Heaven's sweet mercy in his cup,
Can dig, beg, rot, and perish, well content,
So he may wrap himself in honest rags
At his last gasp; but could not for a world
Fish up his dirty and dependent bread
From pools and ditches of the commonwealth,
Sordid and sick'ning at his own success.

   Ambition, av'rice, penury incurred
By endless riot, vanity, the lust
Of pleasure and variety, dispatch,
As duly as the swallows disappear,
The world of wandering knights and squires to town.
London ingulfs them all! The shark is there,
And the shark's prey; the spendthrift, and the leech
That sucks him. There the sycophant, and he
Who, with bareheaded and obsequious bows,
Begs a warm office, doom'd to a cold jail
And groat per diem, if his patron frown.
The levee swarms, as if, in golden pomp,
Were character'd on ev'ry statesman's door,
"Batter'd and bankrupt fortunes mended here."
These are the charms that sully and eclipse
The charms of nature. 'Tis the cruel gripe
That lean hard-handed poverty inflicts,

The hope of better things, the chance to win,
The wish to shine, the thirst to be amused,
That at the sound of winter's hoary wing
Unpeople all our counties of such herds
Of fluttering, loitering, cringing, begging, loose,
And wanton vagrants, as make London, vast
And boundless as it is, a crowded coop.

Oh thou, resort and mart of all the earth,
Chequered with all complexions of mankind,
And spotted with all crimes; in whom I see
Much that I love, and more that I admire,
And all that I abhor; thou freckled fair,
That pleasest and yet shock'st me, I can laugh,
And I can weep, can hope, and can despond,
Feel wrath and pity, when I think on thee!
Ten righteous would have saved the city once,
And thou hast many righteous.—Well for thee—
That salt preserves thee; more corrupted else,
And therefore more obnoxious, at this hour,
Than Sodom in her day had pow'r to be,
For whom God heard his Abr'am plead in vain.

(1785)

# LYRICS

# A SONG OF MERCY AND JUDGMENT

Lord, I love the habitation
Where the Saviour's honour dwells:
At the sound of thy salvation
With delight my bosom swells.
Grace Divine, how sweet the sound,
Sweet the grace that I have found.

Me thro' waves of deep affliction
Dearest Saviour! thou hast brought,
Fiery deeps of sharp conviction
Hard to bear and passing thought.
Sweet the sound of Grace Divine,
Sweet the grace which makes me thine.

From the cheerful beams of morning
Sad I turn'd mine eyes away:
And the shades of night returning
Fill'd my Soul with new Dismay.
Grace Divine, how sweet the sound,
Sweet the grace that I have found.

Food I loathed nor ever tasted
But by violence constrain'd,
Strength decayed and body wasted,
Spoke the terrors I sustained.
Sweet the sound of Grace Divine,
Sweet the grace which make me thine.

Bound and watch'd, lest life abhorring
should my own death procure,

For to me the Pit of Roaring
Seemed more easy to endure.
Grace Divine, how sweet the sound,
Sweet the grace which I have found.

Fear of Thee, with gloomy sadness,
Overwhelmed thy guilty worm,
'Till reduced to moping madness
Reason sank beneath the storm.
Sweet the sound of Grace Divine,
Sweet the grace which makes me thine.

Then what soul-distressing noises
Seemed to reach me from below,
Visionary scenes and voices,
Flames of Hell and screams of woe.
Grace Divine, how sweet the sound,
Sweet the grace which I have found.

But at length a word of Healing
Sweeter than an angel's note,
From the Saviour's lips distilling
Chased despair and changed my lot.
Sweet the sound of Grace Divine,
Sweet the grace which makes me thine.

'Twas a word well timed and suited
To the need of such an hour,
Sweet to one like me polluted,
Spoke in love and sealed with pow'r.
Grace Divine, how sweet the sound,
Sweet the grace which I have found.

I, He said, have seen thee grieving,
Loved thee as I passed thee by:
Be not faithless, but believing,
Look, and live, and never die.
Sweet the sound of Grace Divine,
Sweet the grace which makes me thine.

Take the Bloody Seal I give thee,
Deep impressed upon thy soul,
God, thy God, will now receive thee,
Faith hath saved thee, thou art whole.
Grace Divine, how sweet the sound,
Sweet the grace which I have found.

All at once my Chains were broken,
From my feet my fetters fell,
And that word in pity spoken,
Snatched me from the gates of Hell.
Grace Divine, how sweet the Sound,
Sweet the grace which I have found.

Since that hour, in hope of glory,
With thy foll'wers I am found,
And relate the wondrous story
To thy list'ning Saints around.
Sweet the sound of Grace Divine,
Sweet the grace which makes me thine.

# ODE TO PEACE.

Come, peace of mind, delightful guest!
Return and make thy downy nest
Once more in this sad heart!—
Nor riches I, nor pow'r pursue,
Nor hold forbidden joys in view;
We therefore need not part.

Where wilt thou dwell if not with me,
From av'rice and ambition free,
And pleasure's fatal wiles?
For whom, alas! dost thou prepare
The sweets that I was wont to share,
The banquet of thy smiles?

The great, the gay, shall they partake
The heaven that thou alone canst make?
And wilt thou quit the stream
That murmurs through the dewy mead,
The grove and the sequestered shed,
To be a guest with them?

For thee I panted, thee I prized,
For thee I gladly sacrific'd
Whate'er I loved before;
And shall I see thee start away,
And helpless, hopeless, hear thee say—
Farewell! we meet no more?

# ON A GOLDFINCH,

*starved to death in his cage.*

TIME was when I was free as air,
The thistle's downy seed my fare,
My drink the morning dew;
I perched at will on ev'ry spray,
My form genteel, my plumage gay,
My strains for ever new.

But gaudy plumage, sprightly strain,
And form genteel were all in vain,
And of a transient date;
For, caught and caged, and starved to death,
In dying sighs my little breath
Soon pass'd the wiry grate.

Thanks, gentle swain, for all my woes,
And thanks for this effectual close
And cure of every ill!
More cruelty could none express;
And I, if you had shown me less,
Had been your pris'ner still.


# TO THE REV. MR. NEWTON,

*on his return from Ramsgate.*


THAT ocean you of late surveyed,
Those rocks I too have seen,
But I, afflicted and dismayed,
You, tranquil and serene.

You from the flood-controlling steep
Saw stretched before your view,
With conscious joy, the threat'ning deep,
No longer such to you.

To me, the waves that ceaseless broke
Upon the dang'rous coast,
Hoarsely and ominously spoke
Of all my treasure lost.

Your sea of troubles you have past,
And found the peaceful shore;
I, tempest-toss'd, and wreck'd at last,
Come home to port no more.

OCT. 1780.

# AN EPISTLE TO AN AFFLICTED PROTESTANT LADY IN FRANCE

MADAM, A stranger's purpose in these lays
Is to congratulate, and not to praise.
To give the creature the Creator's due
Were sin in me, and an offence to you.
From man to man, or e'en to woman paid,
Praise is the medium of a knavish trade,
A coin by craft for folly's use designed,
Spurious, and only current with the blind.

The path of sorrow, and that path alone,
Leads to the land where sorrow is unknown;
No trav'ller ever reached that blest abode,
Who found not thorns and briers in his road.
The world may dance along the flow'ry plain,
Cheered as they go by many a sprightly strain,
Where Nature has her mossy velvet spread,
With unshod feet they yet securely tread,
Admonished, scorn the caution and the friend,
Bent pleasure, heedless of its end.
But he, who knew what human hearts would prove,
How slow to learn the dictates of his love,
That, hard by nature and of stubborn will,
A life of ease would make them harder still,
In pity to souls his grace designed
To rescue from the ruins of mankind,
Called for a cloud to darken all their years,
And said, "Go, spend them in the vale of tears."
O balmy gales of soul-reviving air,
O salutary streams, that murmur there,
These flowing from the fount of grace above,
Those breathed from lips of everlasting love!
The flinty soil indeed their feet annoys,
And sudden sorrow nips their springing joys,
An envious world will interpose its frown
To mar delights superior to its own,
And many a pang, experienced still within,

Reminds them of their hated inmate, sin;
But ills of ev'ry shape and ev'ry name,
Transform'd to blessings, miss their cruel aim,
And ev'ry moment's calm, that soothes the breast,
Is given in earnest of eternal rest.

Ah, be not sad, although thy lot be cast
Far from the flock, and in a boundless waste!
No shepherd's tents within thy view appear,
But the chief Shepherd even there is near;
Thy tender sorrows and thy plaintive strain
Flow in a foreign land, but not in vain;
Thy tears all issue from a source divine,
And ev'ry drop bespeaks a Saviour thine—
So once in Gideon's fleece the dews were found,
And drought on all the drooping herbs around.

# THE DIVERTING HISTORY OF JOHN GILPIN;

*showing how he went farther than he intended, and came safe home again.*

JOHN GILPIN was a citizen
Of credit and renown,
A train-band captain eke was he
Of famous London town.

John Gilpin's spouse said to her dear—
Though wedded we have been
These twice ten tedious years, yet we
No holiday have seen.

To-morrow is our wedding-day,
And we will then repair
Unto the Bell at Edmonton
All in a chaise and pair.

My sister, and my sister's child,
Myself, and children three,
Will fill the chaise; so you must ride
On horseback after we.

He soon replied—I do admire
Of womankind but one,
And you are she, my dearest dear,
Therefore it shall be done.

I am a linen-draper bold,
As all the world doth know,
And my good friend the calender
Will lend his horse to go.

Quoth Mrs. Gilpin—That's well said;
And for that wine is dear,

We will be furnished with our own,
Which is both bright and clear.

John Gilpin kissed his loving wife;
O'erjoy'd was he to find,
That, though on pleasure she was bent,
She had a frugal mind.

The morning came, the chaise was brought,
But yet was not allowed
To drive up to the door, lest all
Should say that she was proud.

So three doors off the chaise was stayed,
Where they did all get in;
Six precious souls, and all agog
To dash through thick and thin!

Smack went the whip, round went the wheels,
Were never folk so glad,

The stones did rattle underneath,
As if Cheapside were mad.

John Gilpin at his horse's side
Seized fast the flowing mane,
And up he got, in haste to ride,
But soon came down again;

For saddle-tree scarce reached had he,
His journey to begin,
When, turning round his head, he saw
Three customers come in.

So down he came; for loss of time,
Although it grieved him sore,
Yet loss of pence, full well he knew,
Would trouble him much more.

'Twas long before the customers
Were suited to their mind,
When Betty screaming came down stairs—
"The wine is left behind!"

Good lack! quoth he—yet bring it me,
My leathern belt likewise,
In which I bear my trusty sword
When I do exercise.

Now mistress Gilpin (careful soul!)
Had two stone bottles found,
To hold the liquor that she loved,
And keep it safe and sound.

Each bottle had a curling ear,
Through which the belt he drew,
And hung a bottle on each side,
To make his balance true.

Then, over all, that he might be
Equipp'd from top to toe,
His long red cloak, well brush'd and neat,
He manfully did throw.

Now see him mounted once again
Upon his nimble steed,
Full slowly pacing o'er the stones,
With caution and good heed!

But, finding soon a smoother road
Beneath his well-shod feet,
The snorting beast began to trot,
Which gall'd him in his seat.

So, Fair and softly, John he cried,
But John he cried in vain;
That trot became a gallop soon,
In spite of curb and rein.

So stooping down, as needs he must
Who cannot sit upright,
He grasp'd the mane with both his hands,
And eke with all his might.

His horse, who never in that sort
Had handled been before,
What thing upon his back had got
Did wonder more and more.

Away went Gilpin, neck or nought;
Away went hat and wig!—
He little dreamt, when he set out,
Of running such a rig!

The wind did blow, the cloak did fly,
Like streamer long and gay,
Till, loop and button failing both,
At last it flew away.

Then might all people well discern
The bottles he had slung;
A bottle swinging at each side,
As hath been said or sung.

The dogs did bark, the children scream'd,
Up flew the windows all;
And every soul cried out—Well done!
As loud as he could bawl.

Away went Gilpin—who but he?
His fame soon spread around—
He carries weight! he rides a race!
'Tis for a thousand pound!

And still, as fast as he drew near,
'Twas wonderful to view,
How in a trice the turnpike men
Their gates wide open threw.

And now, as he went bowing down
His reeking head full low,
The bottles twain behind his back
Were shatter'd at a blow.

Down ran the wine into the road,
Most piteous to be seen,
Which made his horse's flanks to smoke
As they had basted been.

But still he seemed to carry weight,
With leathern girdle braced;
For all might see the bottlenecks
Still dangling at his waist.

Thus all through merry Islington
These gambols he did play,
Until he came unto the Wash
Of Edmonton so gay;

And there he threw the wash about
On both sides of the way,
Just like unto a trundling mop,
Or a wild goose at play.

At Edmonton, his loving wife
From the balcony spied
Her tender husband, wond'ring much
To see how he did ride.

Stop, stop, John Gilpin!—Here's the house!
They all at once did cry;
The dinner waits, and we are tired:
Said Gilpin—So am I!

But yet his horse was not a whit
Inclined to tarry there;

For why?—his owner had a house
Full ten miles off, at Ware.

So like arrow swift he flew,
Shot by an archer strong;
So did he fly—which brings me to
The middle of my song.

Away went Gilpin, out of breath,
And sore against his will,
Till at his friend the calender's
His horse at last stood still.

The calender, amazed to see
His neighbour in such trim,
Laid down his pipe, flew to the gate,
And thus accosted him—

What news? what news? your tidings tell;
Tell me you must and shall—

Say why bare-headed you are come,
Or why you come at all?

Now Gilpin had a pleasant wit,
And loved a timely joke;
And thus unto the calender
In merry guise he spoke—

I came because your horse would come,
And, if I well forebode,
My hat and wig will soon be here—
They are upon the road.

The calender, right glad to find
His friend in merry pin,
Returned him not a single word,
But to the house went in;

Whence straight he came with hat and wig;
A wig that flow'd behind,
A hat not much the worse for wear,
Each comely in its kind.

He held them up, and, in his turn
Thus showed his ready wit—
My head is twice as big as yours,
They therefore needs must fit.

But let me scrape the dirt away
That hangs upon your face;
And stop and eat, for well you may
Be in a hungry case.

Said John—It is my wedding-day,
And all the world would stare,
If wife should dine at Edmonton,
And I should dine at Ware!

So turning to his horse, he said—
I am in haste to dine;
'Twas for your pleasure you came here,
You shall go back for mine.

Ah, luckless speech, and bootless boast!
For which he paid full dear;
For, while he spake, a braying ass
Did sing most loud and clear;

Whereat his horse did snort, as he
Had heard a lion roar,
And galloped off with all his might,
As he had done before.

Away went Gilpin, and away
Went Gilpin's hat and wig!
He lost them sooner than at first—
For why?—they were too big!

Now, mistress Gilpin, when she saw
Her husband posting down
Into the country far away,
She pulled out half a crown;

And thus unto the youth she said
That drove them to the Bell—
This shall be yours when you bring back
My husband safe and well.

The youth did ride, and soon did meet
John coming back amain;
Whom in a trice he tried to stop,
By catching at his rein;

But, not performing what he meant,
And gladly would have done,
The frighted steed he frighted more,
And made him faster run.

Away went Gilpin, and away
Went postboy at his heels!—
The postboy's horse right glad to miss
The lumb'ring of the wheels.

Six gentlemen upon the road
Thus seeing Gilpin fly,
With postboy scamp'ring in the rear,
They raised the hue and cry:

Stop thief! stop thief!—a highwayman!
Not one of them was mute;
And all and each that passed that way
Did join in the pursuit.

And now the turnpike gates again
Flew open in short space;
The toll-men thinking, as before,
That Gilpin rode a race.

And so he did—and won it too!—
For he got first to town;
Nor stopped till where he had got up
He did again get down.

Now let us sing—Long live the king,
And Gilpin long live he;
And when he next doth ride abroad,
May I be there to see!

# BILL OF MORTALITY (II)

for the year 1788.

*Quod adest, memento*
*Componere æquus. Cætera fluminis*
*Ritu feruntur.*—Horace.

*Improve the present hour, for all beside*
*Is a mere feather on a torrent's tide.*

COULD I, from heaven inspired, as sure presage
To whom the rising year shall prove his last,
As I can number in my punctual page,
And item down the victims of the past;

How each would trembling wait the mournful sheet,
On which the press might stamp him next to die;
And, reading here his sentence, how replete
With anxious meaning, heavenward cast his eye.

Time then would seem more precious than the joys
In which he sports away the treasure now,
And prayer more seasonable than the noise
Of drunkards or the music-drawing bow.

Then, doubtless, many a trifler, on the brink
Of this world's hazardous and headlong shore,
Forced to a pause, would feel it good to think,
Told that his setting sun must rise no more.

Ah! self-deceived!  could I prophetic say
Who next is fated, and who next shall fall,
The rest might then seem privileged to play;
But, naming none, the voice now speaks to all.

Observe the dappled foresters, how light
They bound, and airy, o'er the sunny glade:
One falls—the rest, wide scattered with affright,
Vanish at once into the thickest shade.

Had we their wisdom, should we, often warned,
Still need repeated warnings and at last,
A thousand awful admonitions scorn'd,
Die self-accused of life run all to waste?

Sad waste! for which no after-thrift atones:
The grave admits no cure for guilt or sin;
Dewdrops may deck the turf that hides the bones,
But tears of godly grief ne'er flow within.

Learn then, ye living! by the mouths be taught
Of all these sepulchres, instruction true,
That, soon or late, death also is your lot;
And the next op'ning grave may yawn for you.

# BILL OF MORTALITY(III)

for the year 1789.

*Placidâque ibi demum morte quievit.*—Virg.

*There calm at length he breathed his soul away.*

"Oh most delightful hour by man
Experienced here below;
The hour that terminates his span,
His folly and his woe.

"Worlds should not bribe me back to tread
Again life's dreary waste;
To see again my day o'erspread
With all the gloomy past.

"My home, henceforth, is in the skies,
Earth, seas, and sun adieu;
All heaven unfolded to my eyes,
I have no sight for you."

So spake Aspatio, firm possest
Of faith's supporting rod;
Then breathed his soul into its rest,
The bosom of his God.

He was a man among the few
Sincere on Virtue's side,
And all his strength from Scripture drew,
To hourly use applied.

That rule he prized, by that he fear'd,
He hated, hoped, and loved,
Nor ever frown'd, or sad appear'd,
But when his heart had roved.

For he was frail as thou or I,
And evil felt within,
But when he felt it, heaved a sigh,
And loathed the thought of sin.

Such lived Aspatio, and at last
Call'd up from earth to heaven,
The gulf of death triumphant pass'd,
By gales of blessing driven.

*His* joys be *mine*, each reader cries,
When my last hour arrives:
They shall be yours, my verse replies,
Such ONLY be your lives.

# SONNET TO WILLIAM WILBERFORCE, ESQ.

THY country, Wilberforce, with just disdain,
Hears thee, by cruel men and impious, called
Fanatic, for thy zeal to loose th' enthralled
From exile, public sale, and slav'ry's chain.
Friend of the poor, the wronged, the fetter-gall'd,
Fear not lest labour such as thine be vain!
Thou hast achieved a part; hast gained the ear
Of Britain's senate to thy glorious cause;
Hope smiles, joy springs, and, though cold caution pause
And weave delay, the better hour is near
That shall remunerate thy toils severe,
By peace for Afric, fenced with British laws.
Enjoy what thou hast won, esteem and love
From all the just on earth, and all the blest above!

APRIL 16, 1792

# PITY FOR POOR AFRICANS

*Video meliora proboque,*
*Deteriora sequor.*

I OWN I am shock'd at the purchase of slaves,
And fear those who buy them and sell them are knaves;
What I hear of their hardships, their tortures, and groans,
Is almost enough to draw pity from stones.

I pity them greatly, but I must be mum,
For how could we do without sugar and rum?

Especially sugar, so needful we see?
What, give up our desserts, our coffee, and tea!

Besides, if we do, the French, Dutch, and Danes
Will heartily thank us, no doubt, for our pains;
If we do not buy the poor creatures, they will,
And tortures and groans will be multiplied still.

If foreigners likewise would give up the trade,
Much more in behalf of your wish might be said;
But, while they get riches by purchasing blacks,
Pray tell me why we may not also go snacks?

Your scruples and arguments bring to my mind
A story so pat, you may think it is coin'd,
On purpose to answer you, out of my mint;
But, I can assure you, I saw it in print.

A youngster at school, more sedate than the rest,
Had once his integrity put to the test;
His comrades had plotted an orchard to rob,
And asked him to go and assist in the job.

He was shocked, sir, like you, and answered—"Oh, no!
What! rob our good neighbour! I pray you, don't go;
Besides, the man's poor, his orchard's his bread,
Then think of his children, for they must be fed."

"You speak very fine, and you look very grave,
But apples we want, and apples we'll have;
If you will go with us, you shall have a share,
If not, you shall have neither apple nor pear."

They spoke, and Tom pondered—"I see they will go:
Poor man! what a pity to injure him so!
Poor man! I would save him his fruit if I could,
But staying behind will do him no good.

"If the matter depended alone upon me,
His apples might hang till they dropt from the tree;
But, since they will take them, I think I'll go too,
He will lose none by me, though I get a few."

His scruples thus silenced, Tom felt more at ease,
And went with his comrades the apples to seize;
He blamed and protested, but joined in the plan;
He shared in the plunder, but pitied the man.

# ON THE RECEIPT OF MY MOTHER'S PICTURE

*out of Norfolk, the gift of my cousin, Ann Bodham.*

OH THAT those lips had language! Life has passed
With me but roughly since I heard thee last.
Those lips are thine—thy own sweet smile I see,
The same that oft in childhood solaced me;
Voice only fails, else, how distinct they say,
"Grieve not, my child, chase all thy fears away!"
The meek intelligence of those dear eyes
(Blest be the art that can immortalize,
The art that baffles Time's tyrannic claim
To quench it) here shines on me still the same.

Faithful remembrancer of one so dear,
O welcome guest, though unexpected, here!
Who bidst me honour with an artless song,
Affectionate, a mother lost so long.
I will obey, not willingly alone,
But gladly, as the precept were her own;
And, while that face renews my filial grief,
Fancy shall weave a charm for my relief—
Shall steep me in Elysian reverie,
A momentary dream, that thou art she.

My mother! when I learned that thou wast dead,
Say, wast thou conscious of the tears I shed?
Hovered thy spirit o'er thy sorrowing son,
Wretch even then, life's journey just begun?
Perhaps thou gavest me, though unseen, a kiss;
Perhaps a tear, if souls can weep in bliss—
Ah, that maternal smile! it answers—Yes.
I heard the bell tolled on thy burial day,
I saw the hearse that bore thee slow away,
And turning from my nurs'ry window, drew
A long, long sigh, and wept a last adieu!
But was it such?—It was.—Where thou art gone,
Adieus and farewells are a sound unknown.
May I but meet thee on that peaceful shore,
The parting word shall pass my lips no more!
Thy maidens, grieved themselves at my concern,
Oft gave me promise of thy quick return.
What ardently I wished, I long believed,
And, disappointed still, was still deceived;
By disappointment every day beguiled,
Dupe of to-morrow even from a child.
Thus many a sad to-morrow came and went,
Till, all my stock of infant sorrow spent,
I learned at last submission to my lot;
But, though I less deplored thee, ne'er forgot.

Where once we dwelt our name is heard no more,
Children not thine have trod my nurs'ry floor;

And where the gardener Robin, day by day,
Drew me to school along the public way,
Delighted with my bauble coach, and wrapt
In scarlet mantle warm, and velvet capt,
'Tis now become a history little known,
That once we call'd the past'ral house our own.
Short-lived possession! but the record fair,
That memory keeps of all thy kindness there,
Still outlives many a storm, that has effaced
A thousand other themes less deeply traced.
Thy nightly visits to my chamber made,
That thou mightst know me safe and warmly laid;
Thy morning bounties ere I left my home,
The biscuit, or confectionary plum;
The fragrant waters on my cheeks bestow'd
By thy own hand, till fresh they shone and glow'd;
All this, and more endearing still than all,
Thy constant flow of love that knew no fall,
Ne'er roughened by those cataracts and breaks
That humour interposed too often makes;
All this still legible in mem'ry's page,
And still to be so to my latest age,
Adds joy to duty, makes me glad to pay
Such honours to thee as my numbers may;
Perhaps a frail memorial, but sincere,
Not scorned in heaven, though little noticed here.

Could Time, his flight reversed, restore the hours,
When, playing with thy vesture's tissued flow'rs,
The violet, the pink, and jessamine,
I prick'd them into paper with a pin,
(And thou wast happier than myself the while,
Would'st softly speak, and stroke my head and smile),
Could those few pleasant hours again appear,
Might one wish bring them, would I wish them here?
I would not trust my heart—the dear delight
Seems so to be desired, perhaps I might.—
But no—what here we call our life is such,
So little to be loved, and thou so much,

That I should ill requite thee to constrain
Thy unbound spirit into bonds again.

Thou, as a gallant bark from Albion's coast
(The storms all weather'd and the ocean cross'd),
Shoots into port at some well-haven'd isle
Where spices breathe and brighter seasons smile,
There sits quiescent on the floods that show
Her beauteous form reflected clear below,
While airs impregnated with incense play
Around her, fanning light her streamers gay;
So thou, with sails how swift! hast reached the shore,
"Where tempests never beat nor billows roar;"
And thy loved consort on the dang'rous tide
Of life, long since, has anchor'd by thy side.
But me, scarce hoping to attain that rest,
Always from port withheld, always distress'd—
Me howling blasts drive devious, tempest-toss'd,
Sails ript, seams op'ning wide, and compass lost,
And day by day some current's thwarting force
Sets me more distant from a prosp'rous course.
But oh the thought, that thou art safe, and he!
That thought is joy, arrive what may to me.
My boast is not that I deduce my birth
From loins enthroned, and rulers of the earth;
But higher far my proud pretensions rise—
The son of parents pass'd into the skies.
And now, farewell—Time, unrevoked, has run
His wonted course, yet what I wished is done.
By contemplation's help, not sought in vain,
I seem t' have lived my childhood o'er again;
To have renew'd the joys that once were mine,
Without the sin of violating thine
And, while the wings of fancy still are free,
And I can view this mimic show of thee,
Time has but half succeeded in his theft—
Thyself removed, thy power to soothe me left.

# A TALE

In Scotland's realms, where trees are few,
Nor even shrubs abound;
But where, however bleak the view,
Some better things are found:—

For husband there and wife may boast
There union undefiled;
And false ones are as rare almost,
As hedgerows in the wild:—

In Scotland's realm, forlorn and bare
The hist'ry chanced of late,—
The history of a wedded pair,
A chaffinch and his mate.

The spring drew near, each felt a breast
With genial instinct filled;
They paired, and only wished a nest,
But found not where to build.

The heaths uncovered and the moors
Except with snow and sleet;
Sea-beaten rocks and naked shores
Could yield them no retreat.

Long time a breeding-place they sought,
'Till both grew vexed and tired;
At length a ship arriving brought
The good so long desired.

A ship!—could such a restless thing
Afford them place of rest?
Or was the merchant charged to bring
The homeless birds a nest?

Hush!—silent hearers profit most!—
This racer of the sea
Proved kinder to them than the coast,
It served them with a tree.

But such a tree! 'twas shaven deal,
The tree they call a mast,
And had a hollow with a wheel
Through which the tackle passed.

Within that cavity aloft
Their roofless home they fixt,
Formed with materials neat and soft,
Bents, wool, and feathers mixt.

Four iv'ry eggs soon pave its floor,
With russet specks bedight;—
The vessel weighs—forsakes the shore,
And lessens to the sight.

The mother-bird is gone to sea,
As she had changed her kind;
But goes the male? Far wiser, he
Is doubtless left behind.

No!—soon as from ashore he saw
The winged mansion move:
He flew to reach it, by a law
Of never-failing love!

Then perching at his consort's side
Was briskly borne along;
The billows and the blast defied,
And cheered her with a song.

The seaman, with sincere delight
His feathered shipmates eyes,
Scarce less exulting in the sight,
Than when he tows a prize.

For seamen much believe in signs,
And from a chance so new
Each some approaching good divines,
And may his hopes be true!

Hail! honoured land! a desert, where
Not even birds can hide;
Yet parent of this loving pair,
Whom nothing could divide:

And ye, who rather than resign
Your matrimonial plan,
Were not afraid to plough the brine
In company with man;

For whose lean country much disdain
We English often show;
Yet from a richer nothing gain
But wantonness and woe;

Be it your fortune, year by year,
The same resource to prove;
And may ye, sometimes landing here,
Instruct us how to love!

JUNE 1793

# THE RETIRED CAT

A POET's cat, sedate and grave,
As poet well could wish to have,
Was much addicted to inquire
For nooks to which she might retire,
And where, secure as mouse in chink,
She might repose, or sit and think.
I know not where she caught the trick—
Nature perhaps herself had cast her
In such a mould PHILOSOPHIQUE,
Or else she learned it of her master.
Sometimes ascending, debonnair,
An apple-tree or lofty pear,
Lodged with convenience in the fork,
She watched the gard'ner at his work;
Sometimes her ease and solace sought
In an old empty wat'ring pot,
There wanting nothing, save a fan,
To seem some nymph in her sedan,
Apparell'd in exactest sort,
And ready to be borne to court.

But love of change it seems has place
Not only in our wiser race;
Cats also feel as well as we
That passion's force, and so did she.
Her climbing, she began to find,
Exposed her too much to the wind,
And the old utensil of tin
Was cold and comfortless within:
She therefore wished instead of those
Some place of more serene repose,
Where neither cold might come, nor air
Too rudely wanton with her hair,
And sought it in the likeliest mode
Within her master's snug abode.

A draw'r—it chanced, at bottom lined
With linen of the softest kind,
With such as merchants introduce
From India, for the ladies' use—
A draw'r impending o'er the rest,
Half open in the topmost chest,
Of depth enough, and none to spare,
Invited her to slumber there.
Puss, with delight beyond expression,
Survey'd the scene, and took possession.
Recumbent at her ease ere long,
And lulled by her own humdrum song,
She left the cares of life behind,
And slept as she would sleep her last,
When in came, housewifely inclined,
The chambermaid, and shut it fast;
By no malignity impell'd,
But all unconscious whom it held.

Awakened by the shock (cried Puss)
Was ever cat attended thus?
The open drawer was left, I see,
Merely to prove a nest for me,
For soon as I was well composed,
Then came the maid, and it was closed:
How smooth these 'kerchiefs, and how sweet,
O what a delicate retreat!
I will resign myself to rest
Till Sol, declining in the west,
Shall call to supper; when, no doubt,
Susan will come and let me out.

The evening came, the sun descended,
And Puss remained still unattended.
The night rolled tardily away
(With her indeed 'twas never day),
The sprightly morn her course renew'd,
The evening grey again ensued,
And Puss came into mind no more

Than if entombed the day before,
With hunger pinched, and pinched for room,
She now presaged approaching doom,
Nor slept a single wink, or purred,
Conscious of jeopardy incurred.

That night, by chance, the poet watching,
Heard an inexplicable scratching,
His noble heart went pit-a-pat,
And to himself he said—What's that?
He drew the curtain at his side,
And forth he peeped, but nothing spied.
Yet, by his ear directed, guessed
Something imprisoned in the chest,
And, doubtful what, with prudent care,
Resolved it should continue there.
At length a voice which well he knew,
A long and melancholy mew,
Saluting his poetic ears,
Consoled him, and dispelled his fears;
He left his bed, he trod the floor,
He 'gan in haste the draw'rs explore,
The lowest first, and without stop
The rest in order to the top.
For 'tis a truth well known to most,
That whatsoever thing is lost,
We seek it, ere it come to light,
In ev'ry cranny but the right.
Forth skipp'd the cat, not now replete
As erst with airy self-conceit,
Nor in her own fond apprehension,
A theme for all the world's attention,
But modest, sober, cured of all
Her notions hyperbolical,
And wishing for a place of rest
Any thing rather than a chest:
Then stepp'd the poet into bed
With this reflection in his head:
Beware of too sublime a sense

Of your own worth and consequence!
The man who dreams himself so great,
And his importance of such weight,
That all around, in all that's done,
Must move and act for him alone,
Will learn in school of tribulation
The folly of his expectation.


# THE CASTAWAY

Obscurest night involved the sky,
Th' Atlantic billows roared,
When such a destined wretch as I,
Washed headlong from on board,
Of friends, of hope, of all bereft,
His floating home for ever left.

No braver chief could Albion boast
Than he with whom he went,
Nor ever ship left Albion's coast
With warmer wishes sent.
He loved them both, but both in vain,
Nor him beheld, nor her again.

Not long beneath the whelming brine,
Expert to swim, he lay;
Nor soon he felt his strength decline,
Or courage die away;
But waged with death a lasting strife,
Supported by despair of life.

He shouted: nor his friends had failed
To check the vessel's course,
But so the furious blast prevail'd,
That, pitiless perforce,
They left their outcast mate behind,
And scudded still before the wind.

Some succour yet they could afford;
And, such as storms allow,
The cask, the coop, the floated cord,
Delayed not to bestow.
But he, they knew, nor ship, nor shore,
Whate'er they gave, should visit more.

Nor, cruel as it seem'd, could he
Their haste himself condemn,
Aware that flight, in such a sea,
Alone could rescue them;
Yet better felt it still to die
Deserted, and his friends so nigh.

He long survives, who lives an hour
In ocean, self-upheld;
And so long he, with unspent pow'r,
His destiny repell'd:
And ever, as the minutes flew,
Entreated help, or cried—Adieu!

At length, his transient respite past,
His comrades, who before
Had heard his voice in ev'ry blast,
Could catch the sound no more.
For then, by toil subdued, he drank
The stifling wave, and then he sank.

No poet wept him: but the page
Of narrative sincere,
That tells his name, his worth, his age,
Is wet with Anson's tear;
And tears by bards or heroes shed
Alike immortalize the dead.

I therefore purpose not, or dream,
Descanting on his fate,
To give the melancholy theme
A more enduring date:

But misery still delights to trace
Its semblance in another's case.

No voice divine the storm allayed,
No light propitious shone;
When, snatched from all effectual aid,
We perished, each alone:
But I beneath a rougher sea,
And whelm'd in deeper gulfs than he.

MARCH 20, 1799.

# OLNEY HYMNS

*These lyrics were written less to be sung by congregations in a church than to be employed in the personal devotions of the poet and others. It is a curious fact that hymns were not normally a part of eighteenth-century church service, even in dissenting and evangelical circles. Rather, singing was typically then limited to responsory Psalms. Since then, of course, several of the Olney Hymns have been set to music and sung in worship.*

## I
# WALKING WITH GOD
Genesis 5:24.

Oh! for a closer walk with God,
A calm and heavenly frame;
A light to shine upon the road
That leads me to the Lamb!

Where is the blessedness I knew
When first I saw the Lord?
Where is the soul-refreshing view
Of Jesus and his word?

What peaceful hours I once enjoyed!
How sweet their mem'ry still!
But they have left an aching void,
The world can never fill.

Return, O holy Dove, return,
Sweet messenger of rest;
I hate the sins that made thee mourn,
And drove thee from my breast.

The dearest idol I have known,
  Whate'er that idol be;
Help me to tear it from thy throne,
  And worship only thee.

So shall my walk be close with God,
  Calm and serene my frame;
So purer light shall mark the road
  That leads me to the Lamb.


II

# JEHOVAH-JIREH—
# THE LORD WILL PROVIDE

GENESIS 22:14.

THE saints should never be dismayed,
  Nor sink in hopeless fear;
For when they least expect his aid,
  The Saviour will appear.

This Abraham found, he raised the knife,
  God saw, and said, "Forbear!
Yon ram shall yield his meaner life,
  Behold the victim there."

Once David seemed Saul's certain prey;
  But hark! the foe's at hand,
Saul turns his arms another way,
  To save th' invaded land.

When Jonah sunk beneath the wave,
  He thought to rise no more;
But God prepared a fish to save,
  And bear him to the shore.

Blest proofs of pow'r and grace divine,
That meet us in his word!
May every deep-felt care of mine
Be trusted with the Lord.

Wait for his seasonable aid,
And though it tarry wait:
The promise may be long delay'd,
But cannot come too late.

## III

# JEHOVAH-ROPHI—
# I AM THE LORD THAT
# HEALETH THEE

EXODUS 15:26.

HEAL us, Emmanuel, here we are,
Waiting to feel thy touch;
Deep-wounded souls to thee repair,
And, Saviour, we are such.

Our faith is feeble, we confess,
We faintly trust thy word;
But wilt thou pity us the less?
Be that far from thee, Lord!

Remember him who once applied,
With trembling for relief;
"Lord, I believe," with tears he cried,
"Oh, help my unbelief!"

She too, who touch'd thee in the press,
And healing virtue stole,
Was answered, "Daughter, go in peace,
Thy faith hath made thee whole."

Concealed amid the gathering throng,
She would have shunned thy view;
And if her faith was firm and strong,
Had strong misgivings too.

Like her, with hopes and fears, we come,
To touch thee if we may;
Oh! send us not despairing home,
Send none unhealed away.

## IV
# JEHOVAH-NISSI—
# THE LORD MY BANNER
### EXODUS 17:15.

BY whom was David taught,
To aim the deadly blow,
When he Goliath fought,
And laid the Gittite low?
Nor sword nor spear the stripling took,
But chose a pebble from the brook.

'Twas Israel's God and King,
Who sent him to the fight;
Who gave him strength to sling,
And skill to aim aright.
Ye feeble saints, your strength endures,
Because young David's God is yours.

Who ordered Gideon forth,
To storm th' invader's camp,
With arms of little worth,
A pitcher and a lamp?
The trumpets made his coming known,
And all the host was overthrown.

Oh! I have seen the day,
When, with a single word,
God helping me to say,
My trust is in the Lord;
My soul hath quell'd a thousand foes,
Fearless of all that could oppose.

But unbelief, self-will,
Self-righteousness and pride,
How often do they steal,
My weapon from my side!
Yet David's Lord, and Gideon's friend,
Will help his servant to the end.

V

# JEHOVAH-SHALOM—
# THE LORD SEND PEACE

JUDGES 6:24.

JESUS, whose blood so freely streamed,
To satisfy the law's demand;
By thee from guilt and wrath redeemed,
Before the Father's face I stand.

To reconcile offending man,
Make Justice drop her angry rod;
What creature could have form'd the plan,
Or who fulfil it but a God?

No drop remains of all the curse,
For wretches who deserved the whole;
No arrows dipt in wrath to pierce
The guilty, but returning soul.

Peace by such means so dearly bought,
What rebel could have hoped to see?

Peace, by his injured Sovereign wrought,
His Sovereign fasten'd to a tree.

Now, Lord, thy feeble worm prepare!
For strife with earth and hell begins;
Confirm and guard me for the war;
They hate the soul that hates his sins.

Let them in horrid league agree!
They may assault, they may distress;
But cannot quench thy love to me,
Nor rob me of the Lord my peace.


## VI

# WISDOM

PROVERBS 8:22-31.

ERE God had built the mountains,
Or raised the fruitful hills;
Before he fill'd the fountains
That feed the running rills;
In me, from everlasting,
The wonderful I AM,
Found pleasures never-wasting,
And swathed about the swelling.

And Wisdom is my name.
When, like a tent to dwell in,
He spread the skies abroad;
Of ocean's mighty flood;
He wrought by weight and measure,
And I was with him then;
Myself the Father's pleasure,
And mine, the sons of men,

Thus Wisdom's words discover
Thy glory and thy grace,

Thou everlasting lover
Of our unworthy race!
Thy gracious eye survey'd us
Ere stars were seen above;
In wisdom thou hast made us,
And died for us in love.

And couldst thou be delighted
With creatures such as we!
Who, when we saw thee, slighted
And nailed thee to a tree?
Unfathomable wonder,
And mystery divine!
The voice that speaks in thunder,
Says, "Sinner, I am thine!"

## VIII

# O LORD, I WILL PRAISE THEE

### Isaiah 12:1

I WILL praise thee ev'ry day,
Now thine anger's turn'd away!
Comfortable thoughts arise
From the bleeding sacrifice.

Here in the fair gospel field,
Wells of free salvation yield
Streams of life, a plenteous store,
And my soul shall thirst no more.

Jesus is become at length
My salvation and my strength;
And his praises shall prolong,
While I live, my pleasant song.

Praise ye then his glorious name,
Publish his exalted fame!

Still his worth your praise exceeds,
Excellent are all his deeds.

Raise again the joyful sound,
Let the nations roll it round!
Zion, shout, for this is he,
God the Saviour dwells in thee!

## IX

# THE CONTRITE HEART

Isaiah 57:15

The Lord will happiness divine
On contrite hearts bestow:
Then tell me, gracious God, is mine
A contrite heart or no?

I hear, but seem to hear in vain,
Insensible as steel;
If aught is felt, 'tis only pain
To find I cannot feel.

I sometimes think myself inclined
To love thee, if I could;
But often feel another mind,
Averse to all that's good.

My best desires are faint and few,
I fain would strive for more:
But when I cry, "My strength renew,"
Seem weaker than before.

Thy saints are comforted I know,
And love thy house of pray'r;
I therefore go where others go,
But find no comfort there.

O make this heart rejoice, or ache;
Decide this doubt for me;
And if it be not broken, break,
And heal it, if it be.

## X.
## THE FUTURE PEACE AND GLORY OF THE CHURCH
ISAIAH 60:15-20.

HEAR what God the Lord hath spoken:—
"O my people, faint and few;
Comfortless, afflicted, broken,
Fair abodes I build for you:
Thorns of heart-felt tribulation
Shall no more perplex your ways;
You shall name your walls Salvation,
And your gates shall all be Praise.

"There, like streams that feed the garden,
Pleasures without end shall flow;
For the Lord, your faith rewarding,
All his bounty shall bestow:
Still in undisturb'd possession,
Peace and righteousness shall reign;
Never shall you feel oppression,
Hear the voice of war again.

"Ye no more your suns descending,
Waning moons no more shall see;
But, your griefs for ever ending,
Find eternal noon in me:
God shall rise, and shining o'er you,
Change to day the gloom of night;
He, the Lord, shall be your glory,
God your everlasting light."

# XI

# JEHOVAH OUR RIGHTEOUSNESS
Jeremiah 23:6.

My God, how perfect are thy ways!
But mine polluted are;
Sin twines itself about my praise,
And slides into my pray'r.

When I would speak what thou hast done,
To save me from my sin,
I cannot make thy mercies known,
But self-applause creeps in.

Divine desire, that holy flame
Thy grace creates in me;
Alas! impatience is its name,
When it returns to thee.

This heart, a fountain of vile thoughts,
How does it overflow?
While self upon the surface floats,
Still bubbling from below.

Let others in the gaudy dress
Of fancied merit shine;
The Lord shall be my righteousness,
The Lord for ever mine.


## XIII

# THE COVENANT
Ezekiel 36:25-28.

The Lord proclaims his grace abroad!
Behold, I change your hearts of stone;

Each shall renounce his idol god,
And serve, henceforth, the Lord alone.

My grace, a flowing stream, proceeds
To wash your filthiness away;
Ye shall abhor your former deeds,
And learn my statutes to obey.

My truth the great design ensures,
I give myself away to you;
You shall be mine, I will be yours,
Your God unalterably true.

Yet not unsought, or unimplored,
The plenteous grace shall I confer;
No—your whole hearts shall seek the Lord,
I'll put a praying spirit there.

From the first breath of life divine,
Down to the last expiring hour;
The gracious work shall all be mine,
Begun and ended in my pow'r.

## XIV

# JEHOVAH-SHAMMAH

Ezekiel 48:35.

As birds their infant brood protect,
And spread their wings to shelter them;
Thus saith the Lord to his elect,
"So will I guard Jerusalem."

And what then is Jerusalem,
This darling object of his care?
Where is its worth in God's esteem?
Who built it? who inhabits there?

Jehovah founded it in blood,
The blood of his incarnate Son;
There dwell the saints, once foes to God,
The sinners, whom he calls his own.

There, though besieged on ev'ry side,
Yet much beloved and guarded well;
From age to age they have defied
The utmost force of earth and hell.

Let earth repent, and hell despair,
This city has a sure defence;
Her name is called The Lord is there,
And who has power to drive him thence?

## XV

# PRAISE FOR THE FOUNTAIN OPENED

Zechariah 13:1

THERE is a fountain fill'd with blood
Drawn from Emmanuel's veins;
And sinners, plunged beneath that flood,
Lose all their guilty stains.

The dying thief rejoiced to see
That fountain in his day;
And there have I, as vile as he,
Wash'd all my sins away.

Dear dying Lamb, thy precious blood
Shall never lose its power:
Till all the ransom'd church of God
Be saved, to sin no more.

E'er since, by faith, I saw the stream
Thy flowing wounds supply:

Redeeming love has been my theme,
And shall be till I die.

Then in a nobler sweeter song,
I'll sing thy power to save;
When this poor lisping stammering tongue
Lies silent in the grave.

Lord, I believe thou hast prepared
(Unworthy though I be)
For me a blood-bought free reward,
A golden harp for me!

'Tis strung, and tuned, for endless years,
And form'd by power divine,
To sound in God the Father's ears
No other name but thine.


XVI

# THE SOWER

Matthew 13:3

Ye sons of earth, prepare the plough,
Break up the fallow ground!
The Sower is gone forth to sow,
And scatter blessings round.

The seed that finds a stony soil,
Shoots forth a hasty blade;
But ill repays the sower's toil,
Soon withered, scorched, and dead.

The thorny ground is sure to balk
All hopes of harvest there;
We find a tall and sickly stalk,
But not the fruitful ear.

The beaten path and highway side
Receive the trust in vain;
The watchful birds the spoil divide,
And pick up all the grain.

But where the Lord of grace and pow'r
Has blessed the happy field;
How plenteous is the golden store
The deep-wrought furrows yield!

Father of mercies, we have need
Of thy preparing grace;
Let the same hand that gives the seed
Provide a fruitful place!

## XVII

# THE HOUSE OF PRAYER

Mark 11:17

THY mansion is the Christian's heart,
O Lord, thy dwelling-place secure!
Bid the unruly throng depart,
And leave the consecrated door.

Devoted as it is to thee,
A thievish swarm frequents the place;
They steal away my joys from me,
And rob my Saviour of his praise.

There too a sharp designing trade
Sin, Satan, and the world maintain;
Nor cease to press me, and persuade,
To part with ease and purchase pain.

I know them, and I hate their din,
Am weary of the bustling crowd;

But while their voice is heard within,
I cannot serve thee as I would.

Oh! for the joy thy presence gives,
What peace shall reign when thou art here!
Thy presence makes this den of thieves
A calm delightful house of pray'r.
And if thou make thy temple shine,
Yet, self-abased, will I adore;
The gold and silver are not mine,
I give thee what was thine before.

## XVIII

# LOVEST THOU ME?

JOHN 21:16

HARK, my soul! it is the Lord:
'Tis thy Saviour, hear his word;
Jesus speaks, and speaks to thee:
"Say, poor sinner, lov'st thou me?

"I delivered thee when bound,
And when bleeding, healed thy wound;
Sought thee wandering, set thee right,
Turned thy darkness into light.

"Can a woman's tender care
Cease towards the child she bare?
Yes, she may forgetful be,
Yet will I remember thee.

"Mine is an unchanging love,
Higher than the heights above;
Deeper than the depths beneath,
Free and faithful, strong as death.

"Thou shalt see my glory soon,
When the work of grace is done;
Partner of my throne shalt be;
Say, poor sinner, lov'st thou me?"

Lord, it is my chief complaint,
That my love is weak and faint;
Yet I love thee and adore:
Oh for grace to love thee more!

## XIX

# CONTENTMENT

### Philippians 4:11.

Fierce passions discompose the mind,
As tempests vex the sea;
But calm content and peace we find,
When, Lord, we turn to thee.

In vain by reason and by rule,
We try to bend the will;
For none but in the Saviour's school
Can learn the heavenly skill.

Since at his feet my soul has sat,
His gracious words to hear;
Contented with my present state,
I cast, on him, my care.

"Art thou a sinner, soul?" he said,
"Then how canst thou complain?
How light thy troubles here, if weighed
With everlasting pain!

"If thou of murmuring wouldst be cur'd,
Compare thy griefs with mine;

Think what my love for thee endured,
And thou wilt not repine.

"'Tis I appoint thy daily lot,
And I do all things well:
Thou soon shalt leave this wretched spot,
And rise with me to dwell.

"In life my grace shall strength supply,
Proportion'd to thy day;
At death thou still shalt find me nigh,
To wipe thy tears away."

Thus I who once my wretched days
In vain repinings spent,
Taught in my Saviour's school of grace,
Have learnt to be content.

## XX

# OLD TESTAMENT GOSPEL

Hebrews 4:2

ISRAEL, in ancient days,
Not only had a view
Of Sinai in a blaze,
But learned the Gospel too:
The types and figures were a glass
In which they saw the Saviour's face.

The paschal sacrifice,
And blood-besprinkled door,
Seen with enlightened eyes,
And once applied with pow'r,
Would teach the need of other blood,
To reconcile an angry God.

The Lamb, the Dove, set forth
His perfect innocence,
Whose blood, of matchless worth,
Should be the soul's defence:
For he who can for sin atone,
Must have no failings of his own.

The scape-goat on his head
The people's trespass bore,
And, to the desert led,
Was to be seen no more:
In him, our Surety seemed to say,
"Behold, I bear your sins away."

Dipt in his fellow's blood,
The living bird went free;
The type, well understood,
Express'd the sinner's plea;
Described a guilty soul enlarged,
And by a Saviour's death discharged.

Jesus, I love to trace,
Throughout the sacred page,
The footsteps of thy grace,
The same in every age!
O grant that I may faithful be
To clearer light, vouchsafed to me!

## XXVII

# WELCOME TO THE TABLE

THIS is the feast of heavenly wine,
And God invites to sup;
The juices of the living vine
Were pressed, to fill the cup.

Oh, bless the Saviour, ye that eat,
With royal dainties fed;
Not heaven affords a costlier treat,
For Jesus is the bread.

The vile, the lost, he calls to them,
Ye trembling souls appear!
The righteous in their own esteem,
Have no acceptance here.

Approach ye poor, nor dare refuse
The banquet spread for you;
Dear Saviour, this is welcome news,
Then I may venture too.

If guilt and sin afford a plea,
And may obtain a place;
Surely the Lord will welcome me,
And I shall see his face!

## XXVIII
# JESUS HASTING TO SUFFER

THE Saviour! what a noble flame
Was kindled in his breast,
When hasting to Jerusalem,
He marched before the rest!

Good-will to men, and zeal for God
His ev'ry thought engross;
He longs to be baptized with blood,
He pants to reach the cross.

With all his sufferings full in view,
And woes, to us unknown,
Forth to the task his spirit flew,
'Twas love that urged him on.

Lord, we return thee what we can!
Our hearts shall sound abroad
Salvation, to the dying Man,
And to the rising God!

And while thy bleeding glories here
Engage our wonde'ring eyes,
We learn our lighter cross to bear,
And hasten to the skies.

## XXX

# THE LIGHT AND GLORY OF THE WORD

THE Spirit breathes upon the word,
And brings the truth to sight;
Precepts and promises afford
A sanctifying light.

A glory gilds the sacred page,
Majestic like the sun;
It gives a light to ev'ry age,
It gives, but borrows none.

The hand that gave it, still supplies
The gracious light and heat:
His truths upon the nations rise,
They rise, but never set.

Let everlasting thanks be thine!
For such a bright display,
As makes a world of darkness shine
With beams of heavenly day.

My soul rejoices to pursue
The steps of him I love:

Till glory breaks upon my view
In brighter worlds above.

## XXXVI

# WELCOME CROSS

'TIS my happiness below
Not to live without the cross;
But the Saviour's pow'r to know,
Sanctifying ev'ry loss:
Trials must and will befall;
But with humble faith to see
Love inscribed upon them all,
This is happiness to me.

God, in Israel, sows the seeds
Of affliction, pain, and toil;
These spring up and choke the weeds
Which would else o'erspread the soil:
Trials make the promise sweet,
Trials give new life to pray'r;
Trials bring me to his feet,
Lay me low, and keep me there.

Did I meet no trials here,
No chastisement by the way;
Might I not, with reason, fear
I should prove a castaway?
Bastards may escape the rod,
Sunk in earthly, vain delight;
But the true born child of God
Must not, would not, if he might.

# THE VALLEY OF THE
# SHADOW OF DEATH

My soul is sad, and much dismayed;
See, Lord, what legions of my foes,
With fierce Apollyon at their head,
My heavenly pilgrimage oppose!

See, from the ever-burning lake
How like a smoky cloud they rise!
With horrid blasts my soul they shake,
With storms of blasphemies and lies.

Their fiery arrows reach the mark,
My throbbing heart with anguish tear;
Each lights upon a kindred spark,
And finds abundant fuel there.

I hate the thought that wrongs the Lord;
Oh, I would drive it from my breast,
With thy own sharp two-edged sword,
Far as the east is from the west.

Come then, and chase the cruel host,
Heal the deep wounds I have received!
Nor let the pow'rs of darkness boast,
That I am foiled, and thou art grieved!

## LIX

# JOY AND PEACE IN BELIEVING

SOMETIMES a light surprises
The Christian while he sings;
It is the Lord who rises

With healing in his wings:
When comforts are declining,
He grants the soul again
A season of clear shining
To cheer it after rain.

In holy contemplation,
We sweetly then pursue
The theme of God's salvation,
And find it ever new:
Set free from present sorrow,
We cheerfully can say,
E'en let th' unknown to-morrow
Bring with it what it may.

It can bring with it nothing,
But he will bear us through;
Who gives the lilies clothing
Will clothe his people too,
Beneath the spreading heavens
No creature but is fed;
And he who feeds the ravens,
Will give his children bread.

The vine, nor fig-tree neither,
Their wonted fruit should bear,
Though all the fields should wither,
Nor flocks, nor herds, be there:
Yet God the same abiding,
His praise shall tune my voice;
For, while in him confiding,
I cannot but rejoice.

L

# TRUE PLEASURES

Lord, my soul with pleasure springs,
    When Jesus' name I hear;
And when God the Spirit brings
    The word of promise near:
Beauties too, in holiness,
    Still delighted I perceive;
Nor have words that can express
    The joys thy precepts give.

Clothed in sanctity and grace,
    How sweet it is to see
Those who love thee as they pass,
    Or when they wait on thee:
Pleasant too, to sit and tell
    What we owe to love divine;
Till our bosoms grateful swell,
    And eyes begin to shine.

Those the comforts I possess,
    Which God shall still increase:
All his ways are pleasantness,
    And all his paths are peace:
Nothing Jesus did or spoke,
    Henceforth let me ever slight;
For I love his easy yoke,
    And find his burden light.

# THE HEART HEALED AND CHANGED BY MERCY

Sin enslaved me many years,
And led me bound and blind;
Till at length a thousand fears
Came swarming o'er my mind.

"Where," I said, in deep distress,
"Will these sinful pleasures end?
How shall I secure my peace,
And make the Lord my friend?"

Friends and ministers said much
The gospel to enforce;
But my blindness still was such,
I chose a legal course:
Much I fasted, watched, and strove,
Scarce would show my face abroad,
Feared almost, to speak or move,
A stranger still to God.

Thus afraid to trust his grace,
Long time did I rebel;
Till, despairing of my case,
Down at his feet I fell:
Then my stubborn heart he broke,
And subdued me to his sway;
By a simple word he spoke,
"Thy sins are done away."

# HATRED OF SIN

Holy Lord God! I love thy truth,
Nor dare thy least commandment slight;
Yet pierced by sin, the serpent's tooth,
I mourn the anguish of the bite.

But though the poison lurks within,
Hope bids me still with patience wait;
Till death shall set me free from sin,
Free from the only thing I hate.

Had I a throne above the rest,
Where angels and archangels dwell;
One sin, unslain, within my breast,
Would make that heaven as dark as hell.

The pris'ner, sent to breathe fresh air,
And blessed with liberty again,
Would mourn, were he condemned to wear
One link of all his former chain.

But oh! no foe invades the bliss,
When glory crowns the Christian's head;
One view of Jesus as he is,
Will strike all sin for ever dead.

# PRAISE FOR FAITH

Of all the gifts thine hand bestows,
Thou Giver of all good!
Not heaven itself a richer knows
Than my Redeemer's blood.

Faith too, the blood-receiving grace,
From the same hand we gain;
Else, sweetly as it suits our case,
That gift had been in vain.

Till thou thy teaching pow'r apply,
Our hearts refuse to see;
And weak, as a distemper'd eye,
Shut out the view of thee.

Blind to the merits of thy Son,
What mis'ry we endure!
Yet fly that hand, from which alone
We could expect a cure.

We praise thee, and would praise thee more,
To thee our all we owe;
The precious Saviour, and the pow'r
That makes him precious too.

## LXVII

# I WILL PRAISE THE LORD AT ALL TIMES

WINTER has a joy for me,
While the Saviour's charms I read,
Lowly, meek, from blemish free,
In the snowdrop's pensive head.

Spring returns, and brings along
Life-invigorating suns:
Hark! the turtle's plaintive song,
Seems to speak his dying groans!

Summer has a thousand charms,
All expressive of his worth;
'Tis his sun that lights and warms,
His the air that cools the earth.

What! has Autumn left to say
Nothing, of a Saviour's grace?
Yes, the beams of milder day
Tell me of his smiling face.

Light appears with early dawn,
While the sun makes haste to rise,
See his bleeding beauties, drawn
On the blushes of the skies.

Ev'ning, with a silent pace,
Slowly moving in the west,
Shows an emblem of his grace,
Points to an eternal rest.

# LETTERS

# TO THE REV. JOHN NEWTON

August 21, 1781

MY DEAR FRIEND,—You wish you could employ your time to better purpose, yet are never idle. In all that you say or do,—whether you are alone, or pay visits, or receive them; whether you think, or write, or walk, or sit still,—the state of your mind is such as discovers, even to yourself, in spite of all its wanderings, that there is a principle at bottom whose determined tendency is towards the best things. I do not at all doubt the truth of what you say, when you complain of that crowd of trifling thoughts that pesters you without ceasing; but then you always have a serious thought standing at the door of your imagination, like a justice of the peace with a riot act in his hand, ready to read it and dispense the mob. My thoughts are clad in a sober livery, for the most part as grave as that of a bishop's servants. They turn too upon spiritual subjects; but the tallest fellow and the loudest among them all is he who is continually crying with a loud voice, *Actum est de te, peristi!* You wish for more attention, I for less. Dissipation itself would be welcome to me, so it were not a vicious one; but however earnestly invited is coy, and keeps at a distance. Yet with all this distressing gloom upon my mind, I experience, as you do, the slipperiness of the present hour, and the rapidity with which time escapes me. Everything around us, and everything that befalls us, constitutes a variety which, whether agreeable or otherwise, has still a thievish propensity, and steals from us days, months, and years, with such unparalleled address, that even while we say they are here, they are gone. From infancy to manhood is rather a tedious period, chiefly, I suppose, because at this time we act under the control of others, and are not suffered to have a will of our own. But thence downward into the vale of years is such a declivity that we have just an opportunity to reflect upon the steepness of it, and then find ourselves at the bottom.

Here is a new scene opening, which, whether it perform what it promises or not, will add fresh plumes to the wings of time,—at least while it continues to be a subject of contemplation. If the project take effect, a thousand varieties will attend the change it will make in our situation at Olney. If not, it will serve, however, to speculate and converse upon, and steal away many hours, by engaging our attention before it be entirely dropped. Lady Austen, very desirous of retirement, especially of a retirement near her sister, an admirer of Mr. Scott as a preacher, and of your two humble servants now in the greenhouse, as the most agreeable creatures in the world, is at present determined to settle here. That part of our great building which is at present occupied by Dick Coleman, his wife, child, and a thousand rats, is the corner of the world she chooses, above all others, as the place of her future residence. Next spring twelvemonth she begins to repair and beautify, and the following winter (by which time the lease of her house in town will determine) she intends to take possession. I am highly pleased with the plan, on Mrs. Unwin's account, who, since Mrs. Newton's departure, is destitute of all female connection, and has not, in any emergency, a woman to speak to. Mrs. Scott is indeed in the neighborhood, and an excellent person, but always engaged by a close attention to her family, and no more than ourselves a lover of visiting. But these things are all at present in the clouds. Two years must intervene; and in two years not only this project, but all the projects in Europe may be disconcerted.

Cocoa-nut naught,
Fish too dear,
None must be bought
For us that are here

No lobster on earth,
That I ever saw,
To me would be worth
Sixpence a claw.

So, dear madam, wait
Till fish can be got
At a reas'nable rate
Whether lobster or not;

Till the French and the Dutch
Have quitted the seas,
And then send as much
And as oft as you please.

Yours, my dear Sir.

# HIS OWN STATE OF MIND AND PROVIDENTIAL CONNECTION WITH MR. NEWTON

MY DEAR FRIEND,— . . . I am sensible of the tenderness and affectionate kindness with which you recollect our past intercourse, and express your hopes of my future restoration. I, too, within the last eight months have had my hopes, though they have been of short duration, cut off like the foam upon the waters. Some previous adjustments, indeed, are necessary, before a last expectation of comfort can take place in me. There are those persuasions in my mind which either entirely forbid the entrance of hope, or, if it enter, immediately eject it. They are incompatible with any such inmate, and must be turned out on themselves before so desirable a guest can possibly have secured possession. This, you say, will be done. It may be, but it is not done yet; nor has a single step in the course of God's dealings with me been taken towards it. If I mend, no creature ever mended so slowly that recovered at last. I am like a slug or a snail, that has fallen into a very deep well; slug as he is, he performs his descent with an alacrity proportioned to his weight; but he does not crawl up again quite so fast. Mine was a rapid plunge; but my return to daylight, if I am indeed returning, is leisurely enough.—I wish you a swift progress, and a pleasant one, through the great subject that you have in hand; and set that value upon your letters to which they are in themselves entitled, but which is certainly increased by that peculiar attention which the writer of them pays to me. Were I such as I once was, I should say that I have a claim upon your particular notice which nothing ought to supersede. Most of your other connections you may fairly be said to have formed by your own act; but your connection with me was the work of God. The kind that went up with the ark from Bethshemesh left what they loved behind them, in obedience to an impression which to them was perfectly dark and unintelligible. Your journey to Huntingdon was not less wonderful. He indeed, who sent you, knew well wherefore, but you knew not. That dispensation therefore would furnish me, as long as we can both remember it, with a plea for some distinction at your hands, had I occasion to use and urge it, which I have not. But I am altered since that time; and if your affection for me had ceased, you might very reasonably justify your change by mine. I can say nothing for myself at present; but this I can venture to foretell, that should the restoration of which my friends assure me obtain, I shall undoubtedly love those who have continued to love me, even in a state of transformation from my former self, much more than ever. I doubt not that Nebuchadnezzar had friends in his prosperity; all kings have many. But when his nails became like eagle's claws, and he ate grass like an ox, I suppose he had few to pity him.

* * *

I am glad that John is in fact a civiller man than I supposed him. My quarrel with him was not for any stricture of his upon my poetry (for he has made several, and many of them have been judicious, and my work will be the better for them), but for a certain rudeness with which he questioned my judgment of a writer of the last century, though I can only mention the effect that his verses had upon me when a boy. There certainly was at the time a bustle in his temper, occasioned, I imagine, by my being a little importunate with him to proceed. He has however recovered himself since; and except that the press seems to have stood still this last week, has printed as fast as I could wish. Had he kept the same pace from the beginning, the book had been published, as indeed it ought to have been, three months ago. That evil report of his indolence reaches me from everybody that knows him, and is so general that had I a work or the publication of one in hand, the expenses of which I intended to take the hazard of upon myself, I should be very much afraid to employ him. He who will neglect himself cannot well be expected to attend to the interests of another.

# SELF-ABASEMENT—
# "THE TASK" NOT ADVERTISED

To the Rev. John Newton
August 6, 1785

MY DEAR FRIEND,—I found your account of what you experienced in your state of maiden authorship very entertaining because very natural. I suppose that no man ever made his first sally from the press without a conviction that all eyes and ears would be engaged to attend him; at least, without a thousand anxieties lest they should not. But, however arduous and interesting such an enterprise may be in the first instance, it seems to me that our feelings on the occasion soon become obtuse. I can answer, at least, for one. Mine are by no means what they were when I published my first volume. I am even so indifferent to the matter that I can truly assert myself guiltless of the very idea of my book sometimes whole days altogether. God knows that, my mind having been occupied more than twelve years in the contemplation of the most tremendous subjects, the world and its opinion of what I write is become as unimportant to me as the whistling of a bird in a bush. Despair made amusement necessary, and I found poetry the most agreeable amusement. Had I not endeavored to perform my best, it would not have amused me at all. The mere blotting of so much paper would have been but indifferent sport. God gave me the grace also to wish that I might not write in vain. Accordingly, I have mingled much truth with much trifle, and such truths as deserved, at least to be clad as well and as handsomely as I could clothe them. If the world approve me not, so much the worse for them, but not for me. I have only endeavored to serve them, and the loss will be their own. And as to their commendations, if I should chance to win them, I feel myself equally invulnerable there. The view that I have had of myself for many years has been so truly humiliating that I think the praises of all mankind could not hurt me. God knows that I speak my present sense of the matter, at least most truly, when I say that the admiration of creatures like myself seems to me a weapon the least dangerous that my worst enemy could employ against me. I am fortified against it by such solidity of real self-abasement, that I deceive myself most egregiously if I do not heartily despise it. Praise belongeth to God; and I seem in myself to covet it no more than I covet divine honors. Could I assuredly hope that God would at last deliver me, I should have reason to thank him for all that I have suffered, were it only for the sake of this single fruit of my affliction,—that it has taught me how much more contemptible I am in myself than I ever before suspected, and has reduced my former share of self-knowledge (of which at that time I had a tolerable good opinion) to a mere nullity, in comparison with what I have acquired since. Self is a subject of inscrutable misery and mischief, and can never be studied to so much advantage as in the dark; for as the bright beams of the sun seem to impart a beauty to the foulest objects, and can make even a dunghill smile, so the light of God's countenance, vouchsafed to a fallen creature, so sweetens him and softens him for the time, that he seems, both to others and to himself, to have nothing savage or sordid about him. But the heart is a nest of serpents, and will be such while it continues to beat. If God cover the mouth of that nest with his hand, the whole family lift up their heads and his, and are as active and venomous as ever. This I always professed to believe from the time that I had embraced the truth, but never knew it as I know it now. To what end I have been made to know it as I do, whether for the benefit of others, or for my own, or for both, or for neither, will appear hereafter.

What I have written leads me naturally to the mention of a matter that I had forgot. I should blame nobody, not even my intimate friends, and those who have the most favorable opinion of me, were they to charge the publication of "John Gilpin," at the end of so much solemn and serious truth, to the score of the author's vanity; and to suspect that, however, sober I may be upon proper occasions, I have yet that itch for popularity that would not suffer me to sink my title to a jest that had been so successful. But the case is not such. When I sent the copy of "The Task" to Johnson, I desired, indeed Mr. Unwin to ask him the question, whether or not he would choose to make it part of his volume? This I did merely with a view to promote the sale of it. Johnson answered, "By all means." Some months afterward, he enclosed a note to me in one of my pockets, in which he expressed a change of mind, alleging that to print "John Gilpin" would only be to print what had

182

been hackneyed in every magazine, in every shop, and at the corner of every street. I answered, that I desired to be entirely governed by his opinion; and that if he chose to waive it, I should be better pleased with the omission. Nothing more passed between us upon the subject, and I concluded that I should never have the immortal honor of being generally known as the author of "John Gilpin." In the last packet, however, down came John, very fairly printed, and equipped for public appearance. The business having taken this turn, I concluded that Johnson had adopted my original thought, that it might prove advantageous to the sale; and as he had had the trouble and expense of printing it, I corrected the copy and let it pass. Perhaps, however, neither the book nor the writer may be made much more famous by John's good company, than they would have been without it; for the volume has never yet been advertised, nor can I learn that Johnson intends it. He fears the expense, and the consequence must be prejudicial. Many who would purchase will remain uninformed; but I am perfectly content.

My compliment to Mr. Throckmorton was printed before he had cut down the Spinney. He indeed has not cut it down, but Mr. Morley, the tenant,—with the owner's consent, however, no doubt. My poetical civilities, however, were due to that gentleman for more solid advantages conferred upon me in prose; without any solicitation on our part, or even a hint that we wished it (It was indeed a favor that we could not have aspired to), he made us a present of a key of his kitchen garden, and of the fruit of it whenever we pleased. That key, I believe, was never given to any other person; nor is it likely that they should give it to many, for it is their favorite walk, and was the only one in which they could be secure from all interruption. They seem, however, to have left the country, and it is possible that he may never know that my Muse has noticed him.

I have considered your motto, and like purport of it; but the best, because the most laconic manner of it seems to be this,—

*Cum talis sit, sit noster;*

*utinam* being, in my account of it, unnecessary.

Mrs. Newton has our hearty thanks for the turbot and lobster, which were excellent. To her and the young ladies we beg to be affectionately remembered.

Three weeks since, Mr. Unwin and his late ward Miss Shuttleworth, and John, called on us in their way from the north, having made an excursion so far as to Dumfries. Mr. Unwin desired me to say that though he had often been in town since he had the pleasure of seeing you last, he had always gone thither on business, and making short stay, had not been able to find an opportunity to pay his respects to you again.

Yours, my dear friend, most truly.

# SELECT
# BIBLIOGRAPHY

# I. PRIMARY

Cowper, William. *The Letters and Prose Writings*. Ed. James King and Charles Ryskamp. 4 vols. Oxford: Clarendon Press, 1980-1984.

—-. *Memoir of the Early Life of William Cowper,* Esq., Written by Himself. London: R. Edwards, 1816.

—-. *Poems*. With a preface by John Newton. 2 vols. London, 1793.

—-. *The Poems of William Cowper,* 1748-1782. Eds. John D. Baird and Charles Ryskamp. Vol. I. Oxford: Oxford UP, 1984.

—-. *The Poems of William Cowper,* 1782-1785. Eds. John D. Baird and Charles Ryskamp. Vol. II. Oxford: Oxford UP, 1996.

—-. *The Poems of William Cowper,* 1785-1800. Eds. John D. Baird and Charles Ryskamp. Vol. III. Oxford: Oxford UP, 1996.

—-. *The Power of Grace Illustrated: Six Letters to the Rev. John Newton*. London, 1792.

—-. *Unpublished and Uncollected Letters*. Reprint Services Corp, 1925.

—-. William Cowper, *Selected Letters*. Eds. James King and Charles Ryskamp. Oxford: Clarendon Press, 1989.

# II. SECONDARY

Cecil, Lord David. *The Stricken Deer: or, the Life of Cowper*. London: Constable, 1929-1933.

Ella, George M. *William Cowper: Poet of Paradise*. Darlington: Evangelical Press, 1993.

King, James. *William Cowper: a Biography*. Durham: Duke UP, 1986.

Marshall, W. Gerald. "The Presence of 'the Word' in Cowper's 'The Task.'" *Studies in English Literature* 1500-1900 27 (1987): 475-87.

Packer, Barbara. "Hope and Despair in the Writings of William Cowper." *Social Research* 66 (1999): 545-65.

Sambrook, James, Ed. *William Cowper*. London: Addison-Wesley Longman, 1994.

Seeley, Mary. *The Later Evangelical Fathers: John Thornton, John Newton, and William Cowper.* 2nd ed. London: SPCK, 1914.

Soubrenie, Elisabeth. "War and Peace in William Cowper's Spiritual Autobiography: Adelphi." *Guerres et Paix: La Grande-Bretagne au XVIIIe siècle.* Ed. Paul-Gabriel Bouce. 2 Vols. Paris: Université de la Sorbonne Nouvelle, 1998.

Thomas, Gilbert. *William Cowper and the Eighteenth Century.* London: Ivor Nicholson and Watson, 1935.